I Love Yoga

A Guide for Kids and Teens

Ellen Schwartz
Illustrated by Ben Hodson

Tundra Books

Published in Canada by Tundra Books,
481 University Avenue, Toronto, Ontario M5G 2E9

Published in the United States by Tundra Books of Northern New York,
P.O. Box 1030, Plattsburgh, New York 12901

Library of Congress Control Number: 2002117468

National Library of Canada Cataloguing in Publication

Schwartz, Ellen, 1949-
I love yoga : a guide for kids and teens / Ellen Schwartz ; illustrated by Ben Hodson.

ISBN 0-88776-598-X

1. Yoga, Hatha–Juvenile literature. I. Hodson, Ben II. Title.

RA781.7.S39 2003 j613.7'046'083 C2003-900100-8

We acknowledge the financial support of the Government of Canada through the Book Publishing Industry Development Program (BPIDP) and that of the Government of Ontario through the Ontario Media Development Corporation's Ontario Book Initiative. We further acknowledge the support of the Canada Council for the Arts and the Ontario Arts Council for our publishing program.

Design: Blaine Herrmann

Printed and bound in Canada

1 2 3 4 5 6 08 07 06 05 04 03

Acknowledgments

The author would like to thank the following people:
For reviewing portions of the manuscript and providing feedback: Elissa Greenfield, Hannah Milstein, Allison Rosenberg, Nina Rosenberg, Rachel Rosenberg, Bill Schwartz, and especially, for her perceptive and helpful critique, Merri Schwartz.
For research assistance: Gillian Elliott, Marcia Ross, and especially Bill Schwartz.
For interviews and quotations: Alexandra Davis, Elissa Desa, Esta Desa, Jesse Desa, Marissa Desa, Amanda Erickson, Kimberley Green, Cathy Hayes, Justin Hayes, Holly Hynes, Beatrice Massara, Bernadette Rollin, and especially, for their invaluable help, Donna Alstad and Andrea Downie.
For permission to use quotations: Kareem Abdul-Jabbar, Alex Bannister, Sheryl Crow, Eddie George, Geri Halliwell, Tobey Maguire, and Sting.

The author is indebted to the following sources of information:
The Complete Illustrated Guide to Yoga by Howard Kent
Yoga for Children: A Complete Illustrated Guide to Yoga by Swati Chanchani and Rajiv Chanchani
Yoga for Children by Stella Weller
Yoga Journal's Yoga Basics by Mara Carrico and the Editors of *Yoga Journal*
www.nextgenerationyoga.com
www.yogajournal.com

For Maxine, Leon, and Sylvia,
and in memory of Ed.

E.S.

To May and Lady,
for their endless support and inspiration.

B.H.

Contents

So You're Curious About Yoga

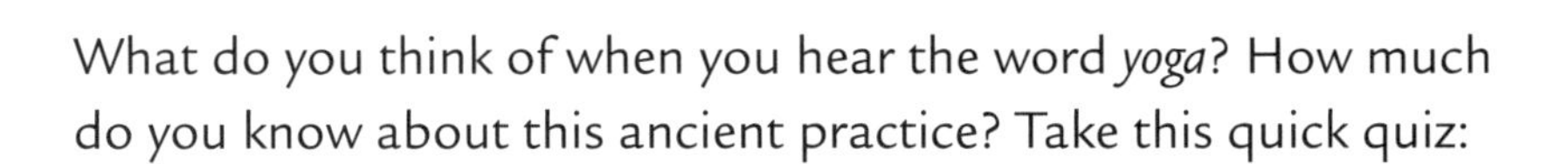

What do you think of when you hear the word *yoga*? How much do you know about this ancient practice? Take this quick quiz:

In order to do yoga, you have to
(a) twist your body into a pretzel
(b) live in a cave, eat nothing but rice and water, and chant funny words
(c) stand on your head for at least an hour a day

The correct answer:
(d) none of the above

Hey, a trick question! Although some crazy ideas about yoga are out there, yoga really doesn't have anything to do with them.

So what is yoga? It's a system of breathing exercises, movements, and relaxation techniques that stretch and strengthen your body, and keep your body, mind, and spirit working together in harmony.

There's an expression that says, "Everything old is new again." That's certainly true of yoga. Although it began more than 5,000 years ago in India, it's a hot new trend right now, and it's being picked up by kids and adults alike.

Did You Know?

- An estimated 28 million people around the world practice yoga.
- Seven public schools in San Francisco have adopted a daily yoga break, and 15 Seattle public schools use yoga as a warm-up in gym class. Yoga is becoming part of physical education programs across North America.
- In 31 states in the U.S., yoga is being taught in prisons, juvenile detention centers, clinics for teen mothers, and schools serving underprivileged kids, to help young people cope, relax, and build self-esteem.
- More than 10,000 people in Mexico do yoga in over 100 yoga classes.
- More and more celebrities are doing yoga to stay strong and focused in their hectic high-pressure lives: musicians like Madonna and Sheryl Crow; actors like Tobey Maguire and Cameron Diaz. And hundreds of athletes, from hockey goalie Brian Boucher to the entire Los Angeles Lakers basketball team!

Why are all kinds of people flocking to yoga? Because yoga makes you feel great! It gives you a strong flexible body and a calm focused mind. It improves your health, stretches your muscles, sharpens your memory, and eases your tension. And it does all these things whether you're six or 60 years old, able-bodied or physically challenged, a jock or a klutz.

Yoga is especially good for pre-teens and teens. It's like first aid for the trouble spots of adolescent life. Yoga can help you control mood swings, help you do better in school, enhance your performance in sports, give you something cool and interesting to do instead of the same old boring stuff, and – maybe most importantly – help you stay calm when your parents are bugging you! And, unlike many other activities, yoga costs next to nothing.

The only equipment you need, in addition to a thin mat or blanket, is your body.

If you're interested in finding out more about yoga and making it part of your life, this book is for you. In these pages, you'll hear from kids like you, telling you why they do yoga and what it does for them. You'll learn where yoga came from and what different types of yoga are practiced around the world. You'll get the scoop on celebrities who do yoga, from movie stars to sports stars. You'll find out how to prepare for your own yoga practice and what pitfalls to avoid. And, finally, you'll get moving with some simple yoga postures.

So, let's go back to our quiz.

Kids like to do yoga because
(a) it's fun
(b) it's peaceful
(c) it's energizing
(d) it's healthy

You got it! The correct answer:
(d) all of the above

So, take a deep breath. Get comfortable. Turn off the TV – the real one and the one in your head, too. Get ready to stre-e-etch, rela-a-a-ax, and feel great!

Get ready for yoga.

Yoga Is . . .

Q: What is yoga?
A: Yoga is exercises. Yoga is breathing. Yoga is relaxation. Yoga is meditation.

How can yoga be all of those things? Imagine that you're making a cake. You mix together butter and sugar, beat in eggs, and then blend in flour and milk. Each ingredient is essential. If you leave out the flour, you won't have much of a cake.

The same is true of yoga. Although many people think that yoga is just a set of movements, it also includes breathing exercises and relaxation techniques. All three parts are equally important. Like the ingredients of a cake, they work together to produce the desired result – in this case, health and calmness, rather than dessert!

Yoga = Union

The word *yoga* comes from Sanskrit, an ancient Indian language, and means "yoke" or "union," like when a pair of work animals are yoked together. So, in yoga, what's being yoked? Everything, that's what! Yoga is designed to unite the body, mind, and spirit. When you do yoga, you hold your body in certain positions, you breathe

slowly and deeply, and you stay present in the moment, paying attention to your body and your breath. When you do all of these things at once, you strengthen your body, focus your mind, and calm your spirit. That's what yoga's all about.

Legend says that the ancient sages, or wise people, of India developed yoga as a way to prepare themselves for meditation. You know how it is when you have to sit still for long periods, like when you're in a boring class or when you're sitting cross-legged. Your legs fall asleep, your mind wanders, and you start fidgeting and wiggling. The same thing happened to the sages, who found that it was hard to sit still while meditating. They reasoned that they needed to strengthen their bodies before they could let meditation work on their minds. So they looked around and observed how birds and animals moved, stretched, and rested. Copying the animals, they came up with a series of exercises to stretch and strengthen their bodies. When they combined these movements with breathing exercises, they found that they could sit longer and focus their minds more easily. Their techniques of body, breath, and mind, handed down through the ages, became the system of yoga that we know today.

The Elements of Yoga

Each element has its own place in the yoga system.

Breathing

Without breath, there is no life. And without breathing, there is no yoga. Breathing is central to yoga. Every yoga session starts with breathing, and breathing is an important part of the exercises and the relaxation too.

If you picture a sailboat scudding across the water, its sails billowing with wind, you'll see the role that breath plays in yoga.

The Sanskrit word for breath is made up of *prana*, which means "breath" or "life force," and *ayama*, which means "extension." So *pranayama* means not only breath but also life, vitality, energy, and spirit – not just the wind in the sails but the energy and force that drive the boat. In the same way, breathing is the life force of yoga.

As you do the poses, you breathe slowly and deeply, with attention. There are also active breathing exercises designed to cleanse the body and strengthen the lungs. Yoga breathing deepens the relaxation your body feels, makes your muscles stronger, and helps your body heal itself.

Exercises

Most people think of yoga mainly as a set of movements like balancing on one leg, or sitting cross-legged, or stretching sideways. And it makes sense that people see it that way because, unlike the breathing and the relaxation, the movements are the part of yoga you can see.

The Sanskrit word *asana* means "pose easily held," and that's what yoga exercises are. They may be slow gentle movements or they may be poses or positions that you hold. (In this book, the words "pose," "posture," "position" and "asana" are used interchangeably.) Many yoga postures resemble living things such as cobras and cats; others copy natural forms like mountains and the moon; still others mimic everyday objects such as boats and plows, or geometrical shapes like the triangle.

Yoga postures work on all parts of the body. They increase your flexibility, strength, and balance, and help you overcome health problems.

Relaxation

Yoga postures may look easy, but they're actually hard work. That's why a yoga session always ends with a brief relaxation

period to rest the body and calm the mind. Relaxation may include visualization (imagining peaceful mind pictures) and meditation (emptying the mind of extra thoughts and focusing it inward). The relaxation portion of yoga restores your energy and increases your sense of calmness and well-being.

Branches of Yoga

In ancient times, yoga was referred to as a tree with six distinct branches, or types. The types are called hatha, raja, karma, bhakti, jnana, and tantra yoga.

Although the branches of a tree are all fastened to the trunk, each one reaches for the sun at a slightly different angle. The same is true of the branches of the yoga tree. They all include breathing, postures, and meditation, but each one takes a different path to the yoga goal of unity.

Hatha Yoga

Also known as the path of physical mastery, hatha is the type of yoga that most people picture when they think of yoga. It's the yoga of activity and movement, the yoga of the postures. Hatha is the main type of yoga practiced in the West, and the type that this book focuses on.

The Sanskrit word *hatha* comes from *ha*, which means "sun," and *tha*, which means "moon." So hatha means balance, the union of opposites. The basis of hatha yoga is the postures, performed with breath control. But, although hatha yoga is focused on the body, it involves the mind too. In other words, you've got to pay attention!

The asanas of hatha yoga fall into five main categories: standing, seated, supine (lying face-up), prone (lying face-down), and inverted (upside-down). Within this framework, the poses may be forward-bending, backward-bending, side-bending, or twisting. That's where the idea of balance comes in. By the time you've done a variety of poses, you've worked your entire body.

Sun and Moon

According to Hindu mythology, when the Sun god Surya married his wife, Sanjna, she could not bear his intense light and heat. She fled into a forest, where she transformed herself into a mare. But Surya was smart – he went after her disguised as a horse! Finally, Sanjna's father decided to help. He trimmed Surya's body, which reduced the god's brightness, and Sanjna was able to live with her husband once again.

The Moon god was known as Soma. He rode through the sky in a chariot pulled by white horses. He was also the storehouse of a magic elixir of everlasting life – also called Soma – which only the gods were allowed to drink. Each month, the gods drank some of the Soma, causing the Moon to wane.

Raja Yoga

Have you ever seen a statue of the Buddha sitting and meditating? He's doing raja yoga, the path of inner focus. The word *raja* means "royal" or "ruler," and raja yoga focuses on controlling the mind for meditation. Raja yoga is designed to take you from concentration to a deeper level of contemplation, and finally to *samadhi*, a state of pure joy in which the self unites with God.

Karma Yoga

The expression "What goes around, comes around" means that the way we act today shapes the kind of life we have in the future. That's the idea behind karma yoga, the path of service. This path

urges us to perform good work, live selflessly, and serve others. In that way, we free ourselves from pain and sorrow, and reach our highest destiny.

Bhakti Yoga

Bhakti means "devotion" or "adoration," so bhakti yoga is the path of devotion. With every action of their lives, whether it's meditating or working in the garden, people who do bhakti yoga try to express their love for God. Think of Mother Teresa, the Roman Catholic nun and Nobel Peace Prize winner who took care of India's poorest and sickest people. She's a perfect example of someone who combines the devotion of bhakti yoga with the service of karma yoga.

Jnana Yoga

Jnana means "wisdom," and jnana yoga involves the pursuit of wisdom and understanding. People who practice jnana yoga read and discuss the classic texts of yoga, seeking answers to the great questions of life.

Tantra Yoga

Ritual is an important part of every tradition. Each Sunday, Catholics recite the Latin mass. On Hanukkah, Jews light an eight-branched candlestick. So it is with tantra yoga, the path of sacred ritual. By observing rituals, people who do tantra yoga try to make everything they do sacred, even the smallest actions and thoughts. One form of tantra yoga is *mantra* yoga, in which people chant a word or sound over and over, aloud or silently, as a point of concentration.

Styles of Hatha Yoga

If you look in your telephone book under *Yoga*, you may find listings for "Iyengar yoga," "Ashtanga yoga" or "Integral yoga." These are different styles of hatha yoga. All are based on the same classic asanas, but each has a different twist. One may focus on the proper alignment of the body, another may emphasize strength, and yet another may concentrate on breathing. With so many types of yoga to choose from, there's a style to suit everyone. Try a variety of classes until you find the pace and approach that are right for you. Here are the most common styles of hatha yoga.

Iyengar yoga

Developed by a famous teacher named B.K.S. Iyengar, this style of yoga pays more attention to the proper placement of the body and less to breathing. Iyengar yoga uses props, such as blocks and straps, to help stiff or weak people stretch farther and get more out of the postures.

Ashtanga yoga

Do you like to move fast? Then Ashtanga yoga is for you. Often called "power yoga," Ashtanga moves through the postures rapidly and forcefully to build strength, flexibility, and stamina. Not surprisingly, it's the style of yoga many athletes prefer.

Viniyoga

Slower-paced than Ashtanga yoga, Viniyoga puts the emphasis on breathing. Using a step-by-step approach, it adapts the postures to meet the needs of individual students.

Kundalini yoga

What if you were told you had a snake living in your body? Don't worry, it's not a real snake! Some people believe that we have a vast pool of energy coiled up like a serpent at the base of the spine. Kundalini yoga uses breath, postures, chanting, and meditation to awaken and release this powerful energy.

Bikram yoga

Named after its founder, Bikram Choudry, this style of yoga is done in a hot humid room to loosen the muscles. However, many people think that Bikram yoga is unhealthy, and it is not recommended for children.

Integral yoga

Instead of confining yoga to a certain time of day, the Integral path tries to blend yoga into a person's entire life. Using a set pattern of postures, relaxation, breathing, and meditation, it aims to make ease of body and peace of mind part of everyday life.

A Word About Other Practices

If you do other activities, such as aerobics, tai chi chuan, or karate, you might be wondering how yoga fits in with them. The answer is "just fine." Each discipline has its own strengths. Some emphasize the physical workout while others place more importance on meditation. Some rev you up and others calm you down. Most of the martial arts have a spiritual component that involves concentration and respect for oneself and others. Yoga fits in with all of them: the physical and the mental, the energetic and the peaceful.

Doing yoga doesn't mean that you can't pursue other forms of exercise. In fact, yoga blends very well with other practices. Although yoga stretches and tones your body, it doesn't give your heart a full workout, so it's a good idea to combine yoga with vigorous activities like aerobics, sports, martial arts, and dance. And yoga is a perfect introduction to quieter pursuits like meditation. It all depends on what interests you. One thing's for sure: yoga is a great way to stretch, build strength, and relax – and that goes well with just about anything!

Yoga and You

Why Do Kids Do Yoga?

Jesse, 20: *When I was growing up, I always thought my mother was weird. I'd come home and find her in the living room in these strange positions. Then I finally figured out what it was all about and started doing yoga. Now it's taken over my life!*

Anne, 13: *I wasn't really interested in yoga – I just went to a class to keep my best friend company. But I loved it! It was so relaxing and so much fun. My friend dropped out and I kept going. That was a year ago and I'm still going strong!*

Talk to ten kids who do yoga, and you'll get ten different reasons why they like it. But their responses boil down to one simple fact: yoga makes them feel great!

Here's what kids have to say about what yoga helps them do.

Feel Good

Natalie, 15: *I'd always been fairly athletic, but my body was stiff. Bending over, I couldn't even touch the floor. Then I started taking yoga. Within a month I was reaching the floor, and now my head's practically touching my knees!*

For many kids, the attraction of yoga is how good it makes their bodies feel. They say yoga makes them stronger, looser, and healthier. Consider all the good things that yoga can do for your body:

- It improves your blood circulation, breathing, and digestion. Got asthma, headaches, sinus problems, or stomach troubles? Yoga's good for them all.
- It stimulates your nerves and glands. That means that yoga can balance those pesky mood swings, and help you grow and develop properly.
- It strengthens your muscles and bones, and makes your spine and joints more flexible. In other words, it makes your whole frame stronger and more elastic. The benefits? Better posture, firmer muscles, and fewer backaches and sore joints.
- Let's face it: between TV, computer games, and the Internet, lots of kids are couch potatoes. That sedentary life can be unhealthy. Yoga gets you moving – and helps you stay fit.
- Although yoga can't change the shape of your eyes or the texture of your hair, it can help you look better – and feel better about your looks – by improving your posture and giving you better muscle and skin tone.

Yoga and Body Image

While it's true that yoga can tone your body, it's not a weight-loss program, nor is it associated with any special diet. Yoga is not designed to make you thinner or change your appearance. In fact, because yoga brings a sense of peace, you're more likely to be content with your body than to worry about how to change it!

Bonus for Boys

As guys grow older, they develop muscle mass and their strength increases. That's good – but it can be too much of a good thing if they get muscle-bound and stiff. Yoga to the rescue! It adds flexibility to balance the added strength.

Gifts for Girls

Girls are generally more limber than boys but they often lack upper-body strength. Yoga can help them build that missing muscle power. What's more, yoga can soothe painful menstrual cramps and help young women establish a regular cycle.

Yoga and Sports

Michael, 17: *My football buddies laughed at me when I told them I was going to try yoga. Said it was a sissy thing. Then they saw that I could stretch farther in warm-ups and didn't get as tired in practices. Now half the team is doing it!*

Elissa, 12: *Once I started doing yoga, my turnout was better in ballet. And in cheerleading, I could do things I couldn't do before.*

You might think that the calm slow movements of yoga don't mesh with the fast energetic action of football, hockey, or track. But yoga is, in fact, a perfect complement to sports. That's why thousands of athletes, dancers, and gymnasts do it. Yoga increases their strength, flexibility, and coordination – and that helps them perform better.

Because I know my body and what it can do, I'm more elusive now.

Eddie George, Tennessee Titan running back, on how the improved flexibility he gets from doing yoga means he gets injured less and makes him a better football player

Yoga also helps athletes prevent injury and heal faster when they do get injured. In many cases, yoga has helped professional athletes play longer, injury-free.

I think that doing yoga really helped reduce the number and severity of the injuries I suffered during my career. . . . It was yoga that made my training complete. There is no way I could have played as long as I did without yoga.

Kareem Abdul-Jabbar, basketball player, long-time center for the Los Angeles Lakers and winner of six NBA championships

Did You Know?

- Kennedy Ryan, a member of the Canadian Freestyle Ski team, used to experience terrible pain and stiffness after the first day of skiing each season. But once she took up yoga, she found that she had no pain at all through the whole first week on the slopes!
- During the twenty years that the Ohio State University

synchronized swim team did yoga, the squad was Collegiate National Champions 17 times, including 10 championships in a row, and sent swimmers to the Olympics and the Pan American Games. Two Olympic athletes won Silver in 1998, and one won Gold in 1992.

Try This

Take a deep breath. How long can you hold it? Thirty seconds? A minute? World champion free-diver Francisco Ferraras can hold his for eight minutes! Ferraras says that by giving him greater lung power and keeping him calm during dives, yoga has helped him break 50 world records.

For kids who are used to the win-at-all-costs world of sports, yoga provides a refreshing change. That's because it's totally non-competitive. It doesn't matter whether you're the most coordinated person in the room or the least, whether you're bulging with muscles or have arms like spaghetti – you're not comparing yourself to anyone else, you're not trying to be perfect or the best, you're just moving at your own pace. So wherever you're at, you win!

Concentrate and Stay Focused

Molly, 10: *I love to think about the animals and things when I'm doing the poses. Like, when I'm doing Downward Facing Dog, I really feel like a dog stretching, getting ready to play. I love the imagination part.*

It's hard to believe that exercise and deep breathing can increase your mind power, isn't it? But it's true.

Consider all the good things that yoga can do for your mind:

- It improves your memory and concentration, so you can learn more easily and even improve your grades. No wonder class rooms across North America are using yoga to help students learn, study, and relax before tests.
- It relieves fatigue and mental strain. You know that tense exhausted feeling you get when you've been cramming – er, studying – for a big exam? Fifteen minutes of yoga, and you're refreshed and ready to hit the books again.
- It helps you sleep better at night. A toned well-used body is your ticket to a sound refreshing sleep. And on those nights when you just can't drift off, a few minutes of slow deep breathing and relaxation exercises will usually send you to dreamland.
- It fuels your imagination. Funny thing about using visualization when you do the poses – it stimulates the imagination and unlocks your creativity.

Did You Know?

- Talk about concentration: Buddhist monks can meditate while sitting in snow! Yoga and mediation help them gain control over physical discomfort.
- Students in a grade-four class in San Francisco found that doing ten minutes of yoga before a big grammar test helped them do better. According to their teacher, yoga helped them concentrate and relax. Less pressure = better grades.

Stay Calm

Ryan, 12: *I used to get in trouble at school all the time for fighting. Then my mom put me in a yoga class. I don't know how yoga works, but it does. It calms me down. When I get mad, I just do yoga breathing. Now I don't*

get into fights anymore. And you know what – playing outside during recess is a whole lot more fun than sitting in the principal's office!

Alexandra, 19: *As a young teenager, I had some body image issues. I felt completely disconnected from my body. Yoga makes me feel whole. Now I feel more comfortable in my body.*

What if there was a way to feel good about yourself, handle stress, and boost your energy – all without alcohol or drugs? There is – yoga! And the best thing is that yoga gives you tools you can use in all areas of your life, for the rest of your life. Consider all the good things yoga can do for your feelings:

- It makes you feel calm and relaxed. Yoga releases tension and produces a peaceful state of mind. People who do yoga report that they feel less aggressive and upset.
- It boosts your energy. Yoga makes you feel refreshed, recharged, and full of energy – yet calm at the same time.
- It builds confidence and self-esteem. As you master the postures and get better at them – especially the challenging ones – your self-confidence grows and you feel better about yourself.
- It improves self-discipline and emotional control.

Kimberley, who teaches yoga at AlpenGirls, an outdoor adventure camp for girls in Montana: *As the girls do yoga, I see them becoming more conscious of their posture and standing more proudly in their own bodies.*

Did You Know?

- Through an innovative program in the U.S. called Yoga Inside, young people in prisons, juvenile detention centers, clinics for teen mothers, and schools serving underprivileged kids are learning

yoga. It helps them deal with stress, control their emotions, and build self-esteem.

- A similar program called Yoga and Time In puts yoga and meditation on the curriculum of schools for at-risk kids. Students say that yoga helps them feel calmer, stronger, and more able to deal with anger.
- Yoga has also proven to help hyperactive children and those with attention deficit disorder. In some cases, yoga helps these kids avoid going on medication.

Chillin'

- An eleven-year-old girl in Ontario reported that when she was scared to go to the dentist, she practiced her yoga breathing and the treatment didn't even hurt!
- A grade-ten student at a West Hollywood, California school for high-risk kids fell behind in her grades after leaving her foster home. Then she started doing yoga. She found that yoga gave her a way to let out her anger and helped her cope.

Get in Touch with your Spirit

Elissa, 12: *Yoga has helped me have a different understanding. I've learned that everything is peaceful inside.*

Yoga is not a religion, but it does have a spiritual dimension. After all, its goal is to unite body, mind, and spirit. Most people, especially in the West, take up yoga mainly as a way to stretch and strengthen their bodies. But somewhere along the way, they find that their minds are more focused and that their spirits are more at peace. That's the spiritual payoff of yoga. Consider all the good things yoga can do for your spirit:

- It helps you build respect for yourself and others. In a yoga class, when everyone is laughing as they all fall over while trying to balance on one foot, and when everyone is cheering each other's progress, there's a strong feeling of cooperation and respect.
- It helps you appreciate the oneness of all people and all things. In the words of a Canadian yoga student in Vancouver, British Columbia: "Through yoga, I've learned that although we're all different, we're all the same."

Alexandra, 19: *Yoga makes me feel connected and strong. When I'm doing it right, everything is flowing harmoniously.*

Esta, doing yoga since the age of 12: *What I love about yoga is that it's not just the postures, it's a way of life. It's the way I do everything. It's how I work, how I stand in a grocery line. There's always a sense of peace, breathing, living fearlessly, recognizing that we're really all one. Yoga enhances everything I do.*

Five Thousand Years and Counting

Peer back through the mists of time. Imagine a group of people moving slowly against a background of lush green jungle. Picture them sitting in silence, eyes closed, backs straight, thoughts turned inward. Hear their breath sighing in and out . . . in and out. . . .

How It All Began

How did yoga start? Who was the first to think of these practices? No one knows for sure, but most people believe that yoga originated in India more than 5,000 years ago. It was handed down for generations until, in 200 BC, a sage named Patanjali wrote a book called *The Yoga Sutras of Patanjali*, a collection of 196 sayings that explain what yoga is. Because Patanjali was the first person to present these teachings in an organized way, he is considered the founder of yoga.

What's a Sutra?

The word *sutra* literally means "thread," but it has come to mean a saying that expresses a profound truth in just a few words.

Not everyone agrees that yoga started with Patanjali. Here are some other theories:

- It all began with the gods. Legend says that Lord Shiva was the first great yogi.
- It began in Tibet. Ancient Tibetan scrolls dating back as far as 40,000 BC describe practices similar to yoga.
- It began in Central America. Statues showing early forms of yoga have been traced to the ancient Mayans.
- It began in Russia. Yoga may have started with the Aryans, a group of nomadic tribes from southern Russia. Somewhere between 1500 and 800 BC, they migrated to Persia and then to India, where they introduced the concept of yoga.

Who knows where yoga really started? And who cares? After all, when something's been around this long, it doesn't matter who invented it – it just matters that it works!

What's a Yogi?

A *yogi* is anyone who practices yoga, although it is often used to refer to a yoga teacher. If you're a guy, you're called a *yogi* or *yogin*; if you're a gal, you're a *yogini*.

Two Thousand Years – The Short Version

This timeline shows how yoga developed from Patanjali's time to today.

200 BC-200 AD – The Bhagavad Gita, the sacred text of the Hindu religion, is written. It talks about yoga.

Around 500 AD – Traveling yogis bring yoga from India to Tibet, China, and Japan.

Around 1200 – The Sufis, a sect of Islamic mystics, bring yoga westward from India to the Middle East.

Early 1300s – A sage called Svatmarama outlines the main asanas of hatha yoga.

1800s – India becomes a British colony. British officials and soldiers learn yoga – and they like it! They introduce yoga to Britain and Europe, becoming the first yoga teachers in the West. At first, Europeans make fun of yoga. But when people try it, they find that it works, and yoga begins to catch on.

1893 – A yoga teacher named Swami Vivekananda brings yoga to North America with a tour of the United States.

What's a Swami?

Swami is a title of respect given to a spiritual master of yoga.

1919 – Up until this point, most yoga shown in Europe and North America has been raja yoga. Now, a teacher named Yogendra Mastamani demonstrates hatha yoga in the U.S.

Through the 1900s – Yoga spreads worldwide as yogis go on tours, publish books, and appear on television.

1960s and 1970s – Growing interest in Asian ideas and cultures leads to an explosion of yoga classes in the West.

21st Century – More and more people are getting into yoga, from toddlers to seniors. Books, magazines, websites, and videos are spreading the word. People are going on yoga vacations, kids are attending yoga summer camps, and schools are making yoga breaks a daily habit. Yoga is hot!

Famous Yogis

Throughout the ages, great yoga teachers have been instrumental in demonstrating the power of yoga and helping spread it around the world. Meet five of the most famous ones:

Ramakrishna

Talk about multicultural! Born into a poor family in 1836 in Calcutta, India, Ramakrishna rose to become a Brahman, or Hindu priest. Later, he became a Muslim, then a Christian, and at one point he even lived as a hermit in the forest. Using yoga as a common thread, he taught that many paths lead to God.

Paramahansa Yogananda

The first famous yogi to settle in the West, Paramahansa Yogananda moved to Los Angeles, California, in the 1920s. He taught that yoga blends with the principles of all true religions. His life story, *Autobiography of a Yogi*, became a bestseller and is still widely read today. When Yogananda died in 1952, there were no signs of decay in his body – even after 20 days!

Swami Rama

Swami Rama was living proof of "mind over matter." In 1970, doctors at the Menninger Institute in Topeka, Kansas, conducted laboratory experiments on him. Using yoga techniques, Rama showed that he could change his body temperature at will and slow his heart rate so much that it almost stopped!

Indra Devi

Indra Devi was a yogi with star power. Born in Latvia, she studied in India, then moved to the United States. When she opened her yoga studio in Hollywood in 1947, dozens of movie stars became her students. Known as The First Lady of Yoga and as Mataji (a term of respect meaning "mother"), Indra Devi is credited with spreading hatha yoga across America.

Ma Jaya Sati Bhagavati

Known simply as Ma, this guru grew up in poverty in a Jewish family in Brooklyn, New York, where she gained compassion and respect for all humanity. Ma cares for the terminally ill, the homeless, the poor, and anyone in need. She operates a center in Florida where children whose parents have died of AIDS find a loving home.

What's a Guru?

A *guru* is someone who teaches yoga. In Sanskrit, *gu* means "darkness" and *ru* means "light," so a guru is a master who leads us out of the darkness of ignorance into the light of knowledge.

Celebrities Who Do Yoga

It seems like every time you open a magazine these days, you read about an actor or musician or athlete who's devoted to yoga. And the list keeps growing, as more and more celebrities discover that yoga can do everything from keeping them looking good to helping them handle the stress of their high-profile lives. Here's just a sampling.

Musicians

Sheryl Crow
Geri Halliwell
Madonna
Red Hot Chili Peppers
R.E.M.
Sting

Actors

Drew Barrymore
Halle Berry
Nicolas Cage
Courteney Cox Arquette
Cindy Crawford
Penelope Cruz
Jamie Lee Curtis
Cameron Diaz
David Duchovny
Jodie Foster
Richard Gere
Tobey Maguire
Gwyneth Paltrow
Jerry Seinfeld
Courtney Thorne-Smith

Athletes

So many athletes do yoga, it would take a whole book to list them all! Here are just a few.

Australian Women's Field Hockey team
Brian Boucher (hockey)
Chicago Cubs (baseball)
Emily Cook (skiing)
Carlos Delgado (baseball)
Cathy Freeman (running)
Eddie George (football)
Orlando "El Duque" Hernandez (baseball)
Grant Hill (basketball)
Martina Hingis (tennis)
Evander Holyfield (boxing)
Lisa Leslie (basketball)
Phil Jackson (basketball coach)
John McEnroe (tennis)

Mark Messier (hockey)
Miami Dolphins (football)
New York Giants (football)
New Zealand All Blacks rugby team
Yannick Noah (tennis)
Dan O'Brien (decathlon)
Philadelphia Eagles (football)
Portland Trail Blazers (basketball)
Reggie Sanders (baseball)
Annika Sorenstam (golf)
Swedish golf team
Jenny Thompson (swimming)
University of Virginia Men's Football team
University of Virginia Women's Basketball team
U.S. Women's Olympic Hockey team

Star Magazine

Read the latest about your favorite stars! No, not who they're dating – how yoga has helped them!

Stretching for Spider-Man

When actor Tobey Maguire snared the starring role in the action flick *Spider-Man*, he knew he'd have to train hard to pull off the quick agile moves of his arachno-hero character. His secret? Yoga for flexibility, plus a strength-training program for muscle: "I was in pretty good shape from my yoga, and I hit the gym a couple of times a week."

It's a Dog's World

Television actor Courtney Thorne-Smith has three dogs who love to watch her do yoga. Often, when she does Downward Facing Dog, one of her dogs is underneath her, doing the same stretch!

A Heavenly Arm for the Devil Rays

In the film *The Rookie*, actor Dennis Quaid played former major-league baseball player Jim Morris, who became a pitcher for the Tampa Bay Devil Rays at the age of 35. Morris was a high-school science teacher and baseball coach whose players promised that they would work hard and have a winning season if their coach would try out for the major leagues. Morris did – and made the team! So how did Quaid, who hadn't played baseball since he was a teenager, get in shape for the role? He pitched, ran, played golf, and did yoga.

On the Road Again

Sheryl Crow, four-time Grammy award winner, brought a yoga instructor on the road with her during her 1999 Lilith Fair tour, and devoted two hours each day to learning the postures. Sometimes, instead of bowing at the end of a concert, she did Side Angle Pose – just for fun: "Doing yoga on the road was really a life-saver, and a life-changer."

Grace on the Gridiron

Alex Bannister, a wide receiver with the Seattle Seahawks football team, says yoga is fab for football, mentally as well as physically: "Yoga teaches you how to relax your muscles and your mind when [you're] under extreme pressure. It also loosens up my body and helps my flexibility a lot. It saves me from injuries because my body can move and stretch in different ways that were not possible before yoga."

Balance and Harmony

Musician Sting credits yoga with helping him deal with the ups and downs of celebrity life: "What we strive for is balance, and yoga is one of those things that helped me achieve more of it than I would have done. An even keel. I'm happy being more balanced than I was."

Stomach Stretch

Geri Halliwell – formerly Ginger Spice of the Spice Girls – combines yoga with aerobics, kick-boxing, and sit-ups to stay in shape: "Yoga's good for strengthening. With the breathing, it massages your stomach without your even realizing it."

Red Hot Yoga

When the Red Hot Chili Peppers get ready to go onstage, lead guitarist John Frusciante and bassist Flea (Michael Balzary) prepare themselves by doing yoga backstage. They even bring their yoga mats on tour.

Lights! Camera! Action!

Film director Mira Nair not only does yoga herself, she brings it on the set. Nair held daily yoga classes for the entire cast and crew while filming her hit movie *Monsoon Wedding*. When she made *Salaam Bombay!*, she recruited 120 street children to be actors, then taught them yoga to help them concentrate.

Unfrozen Music

World-famous violinist Yehudi Menuhin was suffering from a "frozen shoulder" and couldn't play. He turned to yogi B.K.S. Iyengar, who prescribed a program of gentle exercise and relaxation. Sure enough, it worked, and a grateful Menuhin sent a wristwatch to Iyengar, inscribed "to my best violin teacher."

You Have to Be Hindu . . . and Other Misconceptions

"So you're taking up yoga? What religion is that, anyway?"
"Yoga is a breeze. All you do is sit there and chant funny words."
"Yoga is for girls." "No way! Yoga is for boys."

Ever since you told your friends and family that you were taking up yoga, you might have come up against ideas like these. You may even have had some of them yourself. Well, it's time to bust those myths and misconceptions – and here to do it is Yoga Dude, ultra-cool yoga expert.

Ask Yoga Dude

Q: Dear Yoga Dude,
Everybody says that yoga is a religion. I already have a religion and I don't need another one. Is it or isn't it? *Confused*

A: Dear Confused,
No, unh-unh, nah, *non, nyet*! This is probably the number one WRONG IDEA about yoga. Because yoga originated in India, and because a number of yogis have been Hindus, many people think that yoga is part of Hinduism, or even a religion all by itself.

NOT! You don't have to be a member of any particular faith to do yoga, and practicing yoga does not mean that you are adopting any faith. Nothing in yoga goes against the teachings of any religion. In fact, yoga blends with every religious tradition, and folks of every religious tradition do yoga. So stick with your religion, my Confused friend, and rest easy. *Yoga Dude*

Q: Dear Yoga Dude,

I've heard that, to do yoga, you have to be able to sit in the Lotus position, tuck your feet behind your ears, and stand on your head. What is this, some kind of fitness test? *Stiff*

A: Dear Stiff,

There's no rule that you have to be a contortionist! I mean, if you can do those things, more power to you – but you certainly don't *have to* be able to do them. You do yoga according to your own abilities. For every yoga pose, there are little cheats – er, variations – for people who can't do the classic version. Like – don't tell anybody, okay? – I can't get my palm flat on the floor in Side Angle Pose, so I rest my hand on a book. Well really, a telephone book. Well actually, the complete Encyclopedia Britannica! So don't worry. Just do it! *Yoga Dude*

Q: Yo, Yoga Dude,

Yoga's easy. All you do is sit there and relax, right? What's the big deal? *Chillin'*

A: Yo, Chillin',

That's what *you* think, my icy friend. Yoga may look easy. After all, you park yourself in a position and hang there for a while, right? Well, just try holding yourself up in the Plank for more than a minute. Or try standing as still as a statue as you balance on one foot in the Tree. You may not look like you're doing much when you're in a yoga posture, but your body's working hard.

And when you finish, your muscles will definitely know they've had a workout. Mine sure do! *Yoga Dude*

Q: Dear Yoga Dude,
I heard that, to be a yogi, you have to be a vegetarian. Now, I don't have anything against tofu, but I ain't giving up my burgers! What do I do? *Meathead*

A: Dear Meathead,
Whoever told you that is full of baloney! It's true that many yogis are vegetarians. They're into living gently on the earth and all that stuff, and vegetarianism fits in with that. But you don't have to go on any special diet to do yoga. So, relax, pal. You can chow down on your favorite burger and still be a yogi. *Yoga Dude*

Q: Hey, Yoga Dude,
Kids are naturally flexible, right? So why do I need to do yoga? *Gumby*

A: Hey, Gumby,
Remember when you were a baby and you could suck on your toes? (On second thought, maybe it's better not to remember!) It's true that, as babies and toddlers, most of us were very flexible. Our backs were straight, our knees flopped open, and we could fold ourselves in two. But it's also true that, by the time we hit our teens, many of us have lost our early agility – especially if we spend hours watching TV, sitting at computers, and generally being couch potatoes. You know what I'm saying? Stiff city! But the good news is that yoga can help turn you back into a rubber band. You might even be able to suck your toes again! *Yoga Dude*

Q: Dear Yoga Dude,
I want to do yoga, but my best friend told me that it's harmful for growing kids. What should I do? *Scared*

A: Dear Scared,

Tell your best friend, "Fiddlesticks!" For the most part, yoga is perfectly safe for growing kids. In fact, it's not only safe, it's great for them. BUT there is a need for caution. Because your bones, ligaments, and tendons are still developing, you have to be careful about doing movements that might scrunch your spine or strain your joints. Certain poses aren't recommended for kids or should be done only under the supervision of a trained teacher – preferably a superior world-class expert, like me! For details, check out "Proceed With Caution" on page 47. *Yoga Dude*

Q: Dear Yoga Dude,

I'm a guy, and I'm interested in yoga, but I've heard it's for girls. What's the scoop? *All Male*

A: Dear All Male,

Is yoga just for girls? No way! It's a guy thing, too. *Yoga Dude*

Q: Hey, Yoga Dude,

I'm a girl, and I'm interested in yoga, but I've heard it's for guys. What gives? *Girrrlll*

A: Dear Girrrlll,

Is yoga just for guys? Not on your life! It's groovy for girls too. *Yoga Dude*

Q: Dear Yoga Dude,

I read somewhere that yoga is a great way to get thin. That's fantastic! Where do I sign up? *Scale Sitter*

A: Dear Scale Sitter,

Stop! Forget it! Do not pass Go! Yoga is definitely not a weight-loss program. It's not about shedding pounds, getting bulging muscles, or miraculously changing your body. It's about gently toning and stretching. But you know what? You may find that, as a result of standing taller, improving your muscle tone, and breathing deeper, you look better. And you may feel better about how you look. Cool, huh? *Yoga Dude*

Yoga Is For Every Body

Fill in the blanks:
I can't do yoga because I'm too _________ or not _________ enough.

Sorry, you're going to have to find another excuse! Because the truth is, you don't have to be in perfect physical shape to do yoga. Fit or flabby; able-bodied or physically challenged; an athlete or someone who hates sports; underweight, overweight, or middleweight; stiff as a board or elastic as rubber – yoga will work for you if you are simply alive and breathing. You start wherever your abilities are and go from there; the goal is to help you reach the full potential of your body and mind, whatever that potential is. (For tips on how to adapt the yoga postures if you have physical disabilities, see the chapter "Adapting Yoga for You.")

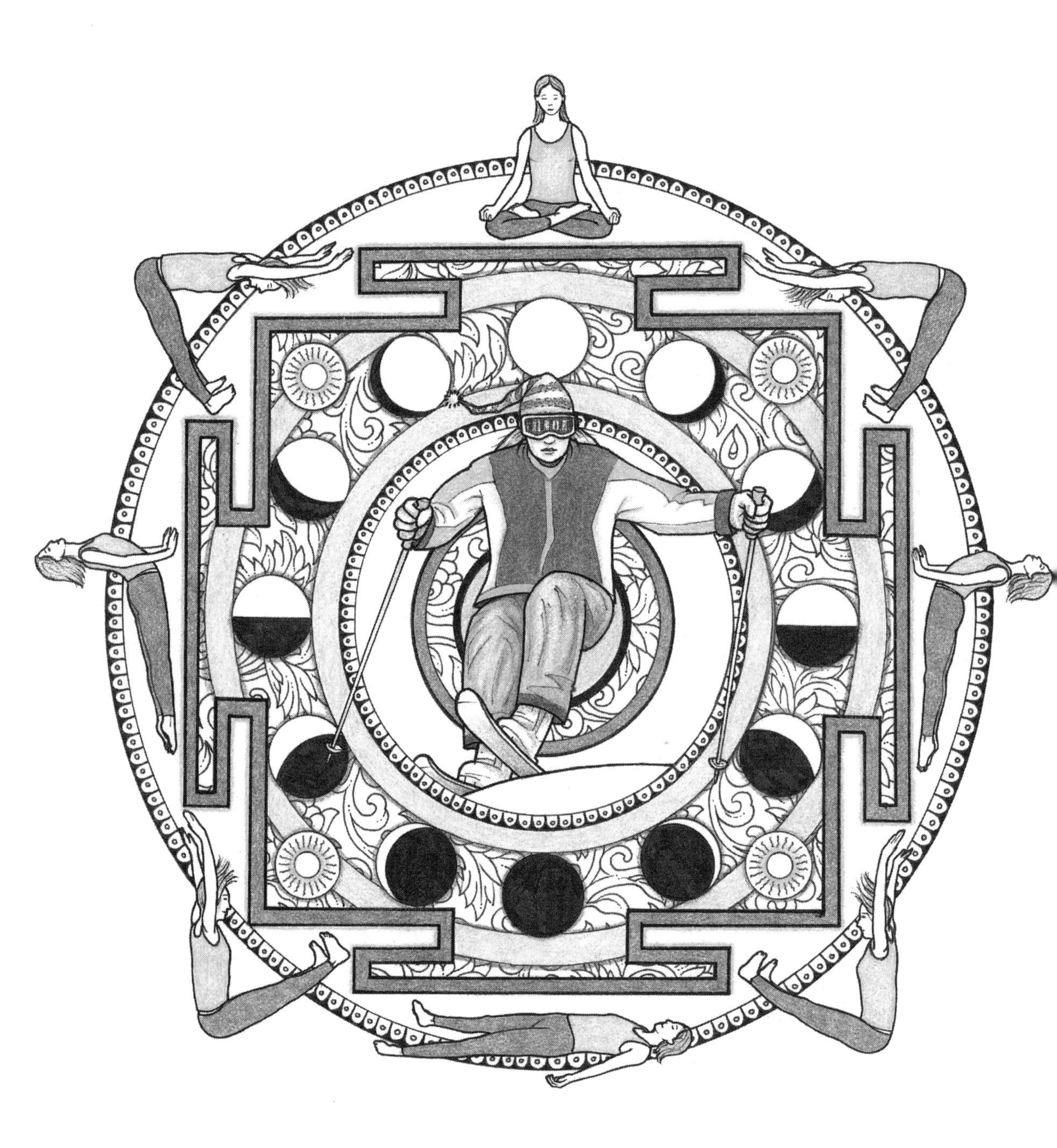

Taking the Plunge

So far, so good. You've been checking out yoga and it looks interesting. You think yoga might be for you, you think you want to try it . . . but you're not sure. Maybe you feel you need more information. That's valid. The old saying "Look before you leap" is there for a reason, right?

Be a Yoga Sleuth

So, gather more information. There are lots of ways to go about this:

- Check out the books, magazines, and websites listed in "Resources" (page 116). They're loaded with info about different types of yoga; the poses, courses, and programs; how to prepare; what to do if you have health concerns, and so on. Some of the websites allow you to post questions and have them answered by experts.
- Talk to friends or acquaintances who do yoga. There's nothing like picking the brain of someone you know.
- Talk to your gym teacher, dance teacher, or sports coach. Many will know about yoga and will be able to refer you to local classes, teachers, and resources.

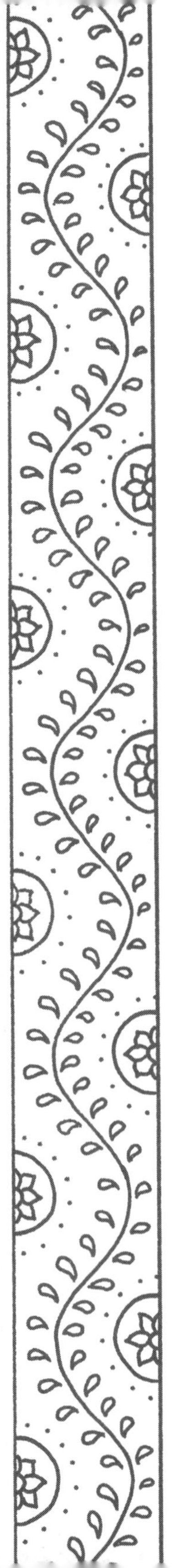

- Call your local community, recreation, or fitness center and talk to different yoga teachers. They'll be happy to answer your questions about yoga in general and about their programs in particular.

Group or Solo?

Okay, now that you've looked into it more, you're sure that you want to do yoga. Good for you! You're going to love it. But wait. Now you have a decision to make: should you take a class or do it on your own?

Don't sweat it. Either is okay. You can learn yoga and benefit from it whether you do it with others or all by yourself. It's just a matter of preference.

Class Act

There are lots of good reasons to take a class:

- It's fun to do yoga with other people.
- You get instruction in how to do the poses properly. This is especially important at the beginning when you're first learning them.
- Your teacher can correct any mistakes or bad habits.
- You're likely to advance more quickly when you have a good model to follow.
- You can do some poses with a partner.
- It gives you discipline. Let's face it: if you have a class, you'll do your yoga!

Finding the Right Class for You

Suppose you decide to take a class. How do you find one in your community?

- Check at your local community, recreation, or fitness center.
- Look in the Yellow Pages or other phone directory under *Yoga Instruction*.
- Ask your friends.
- On the Internet, check out www.yogafinder.com. It's a website that helps you find classes and teachers throughout the world.

What if you decide to go the group route, but you're not sure which class is right for you? Call yoga teachers in your area and ask them about their programs. You might want to find out things like this:

- what style of hatha yoga they teach
- how many students are in the class and what the age range is
- whether the class is right for beginners
- how strenuous the class is

If you have any disabilities or health concerns, this would be a good time to talk them over.

Some yoga programs will allow you to observe a class or take one class on a drop-in basis before signing up for the whole course. So if you're not sure about committing to the course, ask if this is an option. But even if you do have to sign up for the whole course, you can usually get all or most of your money back after the first class if it turns out you don't like it.

Don't be shy about shopping around. Talk to different teachers. Observe or try different classes. Sometimes it takes a while to find the teacher and the class and the style that suits you. It's like buying running shoes – sometimes you have to go through different brands before you find the one that feels just right on your feet!

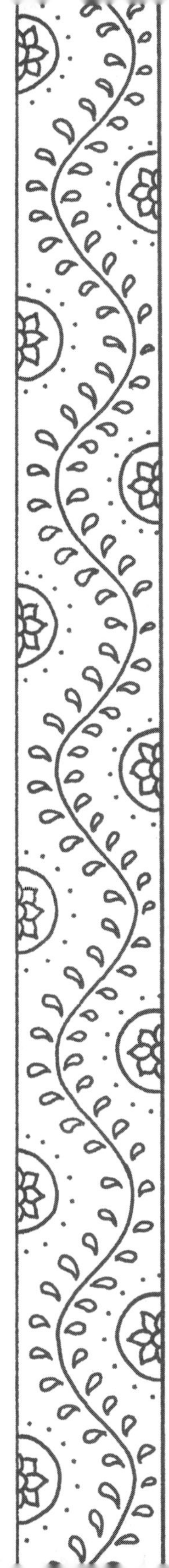

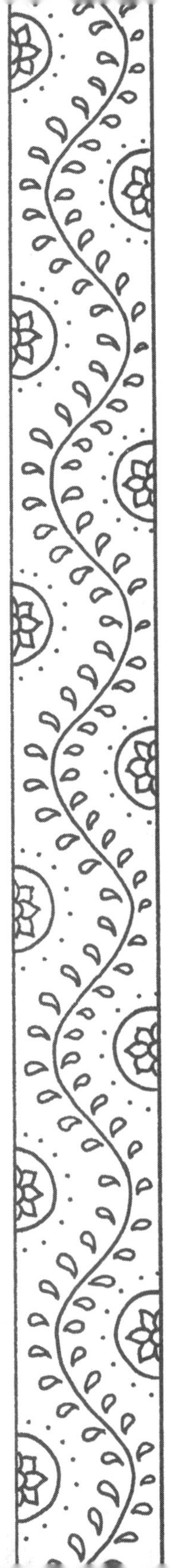

Flying Solo

There are also advantages to doing yoga alone:

- You can design your own routine and go completely at your own pace.
- It's easier to fit into your schedule when you don't have to plan around a class.
- There are fewer distractions.
- You don't have to go to class on rainy or snowy days.

If you live in a remote area, solo yoga practice may be your only option.

If you decide to go it alone, get a yoga manual or video with clear illustrations or demonstrations to make sure you learn the poses correctly. (See "Resources," page 116.)

Who Says a Yoga Class Has To Be Serious?

Amanda, 28: *Sometimes in class, when we're doing Tree pose, my teacher has us close our eyes. Pretty soon, everybody's falling down and laughing their heads off!*

Esta, yoga teacher who has been doing yoga since the age of 12: *Beginners are uncomfortable with their eyes closed. They're always peeking. It cracks me up.*

Kimberley, who teaches yoga at AlpenGirls, an outdoor adventure camp for girls in Montana: *We are often on uneven ground while backpacking, so our balancing postures can be pretty hilarious.*

Twelve Tips for a Safe and Successful Yoga Practice

You've decided to start doing yoga. Now you're itching to get going. But hold on – you can't just jump in there and start stretching every which way! You have to know what you're doing. Follow these guidelines to get the most of out of your yoga practice. (Hint: You might want to bookmark this page – or even copy out the list – and refer to it often, especially when you're starting out.)

1. You can do yoga just about anywhere, but the ideal place is an airy room or patch of level ground outdoors. If possible choose a quiet place where you can concentrate without distractions.
2. The best times to do yoga are in the morning before breakfast or in the evening before bed, but anytime is okay. Try to do it at the same time each day. Aim for at least once a week. Three to four times a week is prefer able, and daily is best of all.
3. It's best to do yoga on an empty stomach. Wait two to four hours after a big meal, one to two hours after a light meal or snack.
4. Do yoga barefoot. Wear comfortable loose or stretchy clothes, like shorts or leggings and a T-shirt.
5. Think slo-mo. Imagine yourself moving in slow motion or underwater, and try to keep your movements just as smooth and slow, both as you do the postures and as you move from one posture to another.
6. Breathe slowly through your nose. Fill and empty your lungs completely, but don't force your breath in and out, and don't hold your breath. (For more information on breathing, see the chapter "Brea-a-a-athe!")

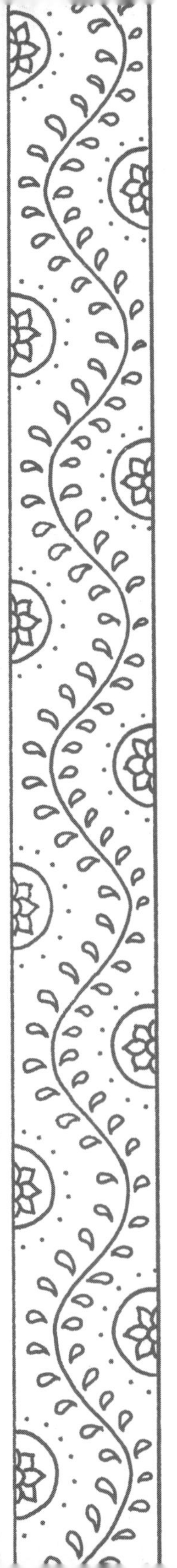

7. Be alert and attentive. Concentrate on the pose you're doing and on your breath slowly going in and out. Pay attention to how your body feels. You can do the poses with your eyes open or closed – whatever feels right to you.
8. As you do each pose, picture the animal or natural form that the pose is named after. For example, as you do the Cobra, picture a snake with its head curving upward, and let your head and back arch the same way. Also, visualize the pose the way you want to do it. When you do the Triangle, for instance, your upper body may not be perfectly horizontal. But imagine yourself doing a perfect Triangle – and pretty soon your body will take the hint!
9. You may do the asanas in any order, but follow the principle of balance. After you do a forward-bending pose, do a backward-bending pose; for example, do the Bridge after Knee Hug. If you twist to the right, twist to the left too.
10. If you're sweating, take sips of water during your session, and be sure to drink a glass of water when you finish.
11. Remember that yoga isn't competitive. If you're in a class, don't compare yourself with others, and don't strain or push to be like someone else. Just go at your own pace.
12. Be patient with your progress. Don't expect to master every pose or to be strong and flexible right away. Progress comes gradually. But it can surprise you too. You may feel as though you're not improving at all, then suddenly you find that you can do something you couldn't do before. You might want to keep a notebook or journal to keep track of your progress – and give yourself a pat on the back for each small improvement.

Kimberley, who teaches yoga at AlpenGirls, an outdoor adventure camp for girls in Montana: *As time goes by, there is a great deal of encouragement and reminders that small changes are happening. The girls become more open and embrace the benefits of yoga because they feel and see the change in their bodies.*

Low-tech All the Way

One of the best things about yoga is that you don't need fancy or expensive equipment to do it. These are the basic tools:

- thin mat or folded blanket (not needed if you do it on the carpet)
- small pillow to raise your bottom for seated postures
- strap or folded kitchen towel to extend your reach
- foam block or thick book to rest your hand on in poses like the Triangle

Special yoga mats are available at yoga shops and fitness stores. They roll up into a nice tight bundle and they have a slightly sticky surface so your feet don't slip. But a thin foam camping pad will do just as well.

Proceed With Caution

Yoga can make you feel wonderful. But just as with any new physical activity, you need to approach it carefully, especially if you have health concerns. Keep these cautions in mind as you begin your yoga program.

- If you have a medical problem, check with your doctor before starting to do yoga.
- When you're sick, don't do yoga. When you get better, start again gradually.

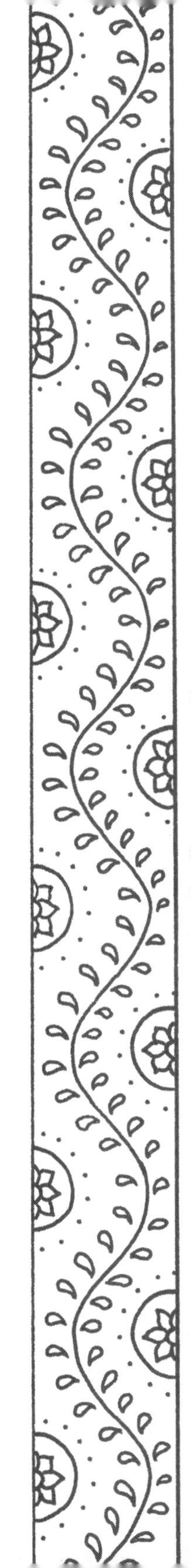

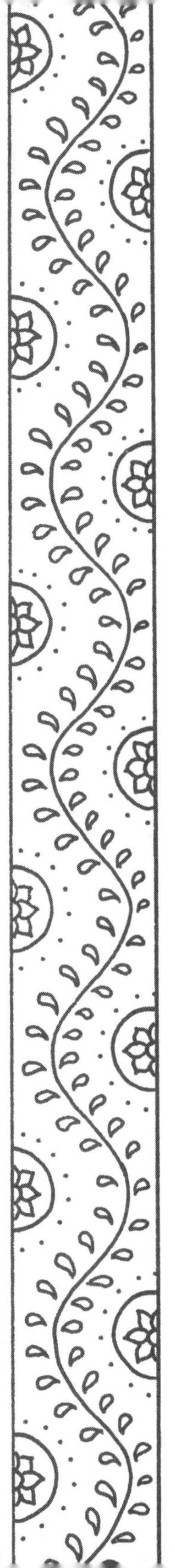

- Have you ever heard the expression "No pain, no gain"? In yoga, the opposite is true. Pain is a sign that you're doing something that's too difficult for you, doing it wrong, or pushing too hard. True, you want to challenge yourself so you keep getting better. So while doing poses, try to stay "at the edge of the stretch," at the point where you're working hard but not in pain. The key is to listen to your body. If it hurts, back off or stop. If you're exhausted, rest. Remember, discomfort is okay; pain is not.
- Don't attempt inverted postures that put pressure on your head, neck, and spine – such as Shoulder Stand, Head Stand, and Plow – without expert instruction. Doing them wrong could result in neck and back strain.
- Avoid these postures if you have these conditions:

If You Have . . .	***Don't Do***
Migraine headache	Shoulder Stand
Back pain	Boat or Shoulder Stand
Chest problems (asthma, bronchitis, etc.)	Special breathing techniques
Heart problems and high bloodpressure	Inverted postures
Varicose veins	Cross-legged postures
Hernia in the abdomen, chest or groin	Forward bends
For girls: Your period	Inverted poses

Get Warmed Up

Think of yoga as a four-course meal:

1. For your appetizer, some delightful little warm-ups.
2. For your salad, a fresh well-tossed session of breathing.
3. For your main dish, the hearty nutrition-filled poses.
4. And for dessert, some deliciously soothing relaxation.

Yum!

Every yoga session should have these four courses. Just as the courses of a meal fill you up and ensure that you get the proper nutrition, the different stages of yoga prepare your body and mind to do the work of the poses and help you get the most out of your yoga practice.

This chapter and the three that follow – "Brea-a-a-athe!," "The Poses," and "Rela-a-a-ax!" – take you through each part of a yoga session.

Warming Up

Just like a dancer, musician, or athlete, you need to warm up for a few minutes before doing yoga to prevent injury and prepare yourself to concentrate. If you jump into the postures cold, you might strain your muscles, or you might be too stiff to get much out of the asanas.

Here are nine suggested warm-up exercises. It's not necessary to do all of them every time – just choose a few or do some of your own favorites. Be sure to vary them so that you work different parts of your body.

Unless it says otherwise, you may do the warm-ups standing up or sitting down. (For tips on standing properly and sitting comfortably, see "A Word on Posture" on page 56 and "Cross-legged Comfort" on page 58.)

Figure Eight: With your head, slowly and smoothly draw a sideways figure 8 in the air. Imagine that, when you are facing front, your head is positioned right in the middle of the 8, where the two halves join. Make sure that you come back to that point in the middle of every figure 8. Do this five times in one direction and five times in the other.

Shoulder Rotation: Roll your shoulders in a big backward circle. Let your arms hang loosely at your sides. They will lift and roll outward, and your elbows will bend slightly, as your shoulders roll up and back. Do this five times. If you spend a lot of time hunched over a computer keyboard or video game, your shoulders may tend to draw forward – this warm-up will correct that habit.

Clock: Holding your head still, look up so that both eyes point at 12:00 on an imaginary clock. Move both eyes to 1:00, 2:00, and so on all around the clock. Repeat, this time going counterclockwise.

Butterfly: In this exercise, your legs flutter up and down like the wings of a butterfly. Sit with the soles of your feet together and your knees bent and hanging open. Hold on to your right instep (the upper surface of your foot, over your arch) with your right hand, and your left instep with your left hand. As you breathe in, draw your knees up under your armpits. Keep your feet on the floor. As you exhale, gently lower your knees. Do this eight times.

Ankle Rotation: Lie on your back with your knees hugged to your chest. Rotate your ankles, drawing circles in the air with your toes. Do this five times in one direction and five times in the other.

Rock 'n' Roll: Sit with your knees bent and your arms wrapped loosely around your legs. Rock forward just until your toes touch the floor, then backward as far as you can without letting go of your legs and without rolling all the way onto your back. Try to keep your knees the same distance from your chest all the time. Rock forward and backward ten times, holding for a moment in each position.

Upper Arm Stretch: Raise your left arm with the elbow bent so that your elbow points toward the ceiling and your hand hangs behind your neck. Bring your right hand over your head and grab your left elbow. Gently push back until you feel a stretch in your left upper arm – don't over do the stretch or you could pull a muscle. Hold for several seconds, then lower. Repeat on the right side.

This stretch is not only a good warm-up, it's great to do after poses that work your arms and shoulders such as Plank and Downward Facing Dog.

Seated Forward Bend: Sit in a chair with your back straight, feet flat on the floor, arms hanging at your sides. As you breathe in, swing your arms up and over your head. Then breathe out and lean forward, collapsing over your legs and letting your arms and head hang loosely. Breathe in and roll back up to the starting position. Do this four times.

Standing Forward Bend: Same as Seated Forward Bend, only you do it standing with your feet a hip-width apart. When you bend over, let your upper body hang down as far as it can; it might even touch your thighs. Let your arms and head hang down loosely, and keep your knees slightly bent. Do this four times.

Positioned for Success

In yoga, there are basic positions and movements that you use over and over, and you'll come across them many times in this book. Here are three of the most common ones. Practice these a few times before you start the asanas so you can do them easily and naturally.

Hip-Width

When the instructions say to stand with your feet a hip-width apart, stand with your feet the same distance apart as your hips,

with your toes facing front. The idea is to make a straight line from your hip, down your leg and ankle to the floor. If necessary, look down and check. After a while, standing in this position will become second nature and you won't need to look.

Rolling Up

Have you ever seen a fern in the early spring when it's all curled up? Can you imagine the fern slowly uncurling until it's completely open? That's the idea of rolling up. It's a safe and gentle way to return to an upright position from a forward bend – and it feels great! Here's what you do. Stand with your feet a comfortable distance apart. Bend over, letting your arms and head hang loosely. Keeping the whole upper part of your body hanging down, start rolling your back up so that your tailbone – and only your tailbone – comes to a vertical position. Then keep rolling your lower back up so that it's stacked directly over your tailbone. Then your middle back. Then your upper back. Then your neck. Finally, let your head float up to the top. Try to make the whole movement one smooth uncurling.

Parallel Hands and Knees

This is the starting position for many prone (face-down) postures. Kneel on your hands and knees with your hands directly beneath your shoulders and your knees under your hips. Keep your palms flat on the floor with your fingers spread apart, and the tops of your feet flat on the floor without your toes tucked under. Keep your back flat so that it is parallel to the floor. Don't raise your head; keep the back of your neck in line with your back so that you form a straight line from your tailbone to the top of your head.

A Word on Posture

Think of your spine as a garden hose. It can't work when it's bent. It has to be straight to let the energy through. The same thing holds true in yoga. It's important to sit and stand straight, whether you're doing the asanas or just warming up. When you start a movement from a straight aligned position, you're centered, you have better balance, and you get more benefit from the movement.

Being straight doesn't mean that you're trying to flatten out your back and neck – they have natural curves that belong there. What it does mean is that the different parts of your body are stacked on top of each other so that someone could trace a straight line from your earlobe to your shoulder to your hip to your knee to your ankle.

How to Stand Straight

Keep your weight evenly balanced between your right foot and your left, and between the front of your foot and your heel.

Try This

Here's a fun way to find this point of balance. With your eyes closed, rock forward and backward, forward and backward, shifting your weight first onto the balls of your feet and then onto your heels. At first, lean fairly far in either direction (but keeping your whole foot on the floor at all times), then gradually make the motion smaller and smaller. Stop when you are right in the middle. Open your eyes.

Now, working upward, imagine that your knees are directly over your ankles, your hips are over your knees, your shoulders are over your hips, and your ears are over your shoulders.

Tuck your chin in slightly and let the back of your neck be long. Let your head rest lightly on top of your neck. Now you're straight!

Using mental images can help you stand straighter, too:

- Imagine that you are a puppet and that invisible strings are connected to the top of your head. Imagine that the pup peteer is gently tugging the strings upward.
- Visualize (or look at) a tree or mountain and feel just as tall.
- Repeat to yourself: I am tall and centered.

Try This

How do you know if your posture is straight? Take these simple tests:

The Paper Cup Test

When you're sitting, place a paper cup upside-down on the crown of your head. If it stays up – congratulations! – you're sitting straight. If it falls off, adjust your posture. As you do yoga, your posture will improve and the cup will stay up longer.

The Wall Test

It's good to do this with a friend so you can measure each other. Stand against a wall with your heels about 1/2 inch (2–3 cm) away. (Your bum may be touching the wall.) With your fingers, measure the distance between the back of your head and the wall. Adjust your posture so that the back of your head is the same distance from the wall as your heels. This is straight. Walk around the room, trying to stay straight. Go back to the wall and measure again. How far off are you? Try again and see if you can stay upright.

Cross-legged Comfort

Sitting plays a large part in yoga. For instance, there are many seated asanas. You might do the warm-ups and the breathing sitting down. And, if you meditate, you might do so in a seated position. So what's the best way to sit?

If you've ever looked through a yoga manual or seen a statue of the Buddha, you've probably seen the Lotus pose. It's that classic and beautiful cross-legged position in which each foot rests on the opposite thigh. (See page 78 for instructions on doing the Lotus.) But the Lotus position can be hard to do, especially if you have stiff legs or hips, and you can injure yourself if you force yourself into it. Indeed, for some people, sitting cross-legged in any way is uncomfortable.

The good news: you don't have to be able sit in the Lotus pose or any other cross-legged position to do yoga. In fact, you may sit in any position that's comfortable for you:

- You could sit in the traditional cross-legged "tailor" position, with each foot tucked under the opposite leg.
- You could sit with one foot tucked into the V between your legs and the other foot resting just outside of the first.
- You could kneel upright with your knees bent and your lower legs under your thighs, so that your bottom is resting on your heels.
- You could sit in a chair.

Try This

When you're sitting cross-legged, put a small pillow or folded blanket under your bottom so that you're tilted slightly forward. This takes the strain off your hips and helps you sit up taller.

Clickety-Clack

As you start to do the warm-up exercises – especially if you've been sitting around for a while or are stiff – you may hear faint clicking noises coming from your joints. Don't worry – you're not falling apart! That's just the cartilage in your joints moving around. There's fluid in your joints, called synovial fluid, that lubricates the joints so that their parts can move without rubbing. When you've been inactive, it takes a few moments for the synovial fluid to start flowing, so the dry cartilage makes a little noise. As long as you don't feel pain, it's perfectly normal and harmless.

On to the Next Step

Now that you've warmed up, you're ready to do a few minutes of yoga breathing to relax, focus your attention, and prepare yourself for the asanas.

Brea-a-a-athe!

Q: The faster you run, the harder I am to catch. What am I?
A: Your breath, of course!

Breathing is perhaps the most important thing you do, yet you probably don't even notice you're doing it. But yoga shows that if you pay attention to your breath, you feel healthier, more alert, and more alive.

Breathing, and awareness of breathing, is absolutely central to yoga. After you've warmed up, you do a short session of deep breathing to calm yourself down and focus your attention. As you do the asanas, you keep breathing slowly and deeply, paying attention to your breath. And when you relax at the end, you use your breath to rest your muscles and restore your energy. So, as you can see, breath is the element that links all the different parts of yoga together.

Go Deep

Breathing is breathing, right? Yes and no. Ordinary breathing is actually quite shallow. If you're like most people, you usually take short shallow breaths, filling only the top part of your lungs.

That means that you're not using your lungs nearly as fully as you can. And that means that you don't take in as much oxygen as you could. It also means that stale air can sit at the bottom of your lungs, taking up space and not doing you any good.

Yoga breathing, on the other hand, uses your lungs fully. It brings in extra oxygen and gets rid of every last bit of stale air. That's why it's so good for you.

Belly Breathing

Yoga breathing is also called "belly" or "balloon" breathing. Here's how you do it:

1. Imagine that you have a balloon inside you, with the round end at the bottom of your stomach and the opening in your throat.
2. As you breathe in, imagine the air filling first the bottom of the balloon, deep in your belly, then slowly coming higher as it fills up the balloon in your upper stomach, your chest, and finally your throat. Put one hand on your stomach and the other on your upper chest, and you will feel first your belly rise and then your chest.
3. As you breathe out, imagine the balloon slowly emptying. Lightly squeeze your stomach muscles to push out every last bit of air. Your hands will fall as your belly and chest empty out.

As you do belly breathing, follow these pointers:

- Breathe through your nose with your mouth closed. Keep your face relaxed.
- Try to make each in-breath and each out-breath as slow and even as possible.
- Breathe in and out as deeply as you can, but don't hold your breath.
- Focus on your breath. Feel it going in and out of your body.

Does all that sound like too much to keep track of? Remember the most important rule of all: When in doubt, just breathe!

Try This

For fun, when you're belly breathing, put something on your stomach, such as a small toy, and watch it rise and fall like a boat riding the waves of the sea.

Breathing Session Before Doing the Postures

Do several minutes of yoga breathing after your warm-ups and before your asanas. This focuses your mind and gets you ready to do the poses.

1. Sit or lie in a relaxed position.
   - If you're sitting, you may sit in a chair or on the floor. Sit tall, but not stiffly. If you're sitting cross-legged, you may use a cushion to help you sit up taller. (See "Cross-legged Comfort" on page 58.)
   - If you're lying down, lie on your back with your legs com fortably apart and your arms loosely out to the sides, palms up.
2. At first, just breathe normally. Simply observe your breath and your body. How does your breath feel as it goes into your lungs? How does your body feel? Are there any tight or uncomfortable spots? Imagine your breath going into those spots and loosening them.
3. Start to lengthen your breath. See how many counts you can make each inhalation and exhalation last. Four? Six? More?

4. Do belly breathing for a few minutes.
5. When you feel relaxed and focused, you're ready to start your asanas.

Now, Pay Attention!

I'm focusing on my breathing. In . . . out . . . in . . . out . . . Oh, that was a pretty bird song . . . Wonder what kind of bird it was. That reminds me – did I remember to fill the bird feeder? . . . Oops, got to concentrate. In . . . out . . . Wonder what's for breakfast. I'm in the mood for French toast, smothered in syrup. Yummm . . . Darn! Mind wandered again. Okay, this time I'm really going to concentrate. In . . . out . . . in . . . out . . . in . . . Wow, look how good I'm doing. If only I'd done this well on my math test. Really blew it. Mom and Dad are gonna freak out – Aarrgghh! Did it again. Now, pay attention!

If this is what goes on in your head when you're trying to focus, don't worry, it's normal. The mind is a stubborn and active creature, skittering from thought to thought. It doesn't like to be empty and still – in fact, it has a mind of its own! So when you catch your mind wandering, don't get mad at yourself. Simply let go of the distracting thought and return to your focus. Gradually – *very* gradually – you'll get better at concentrating.

Yoga Breathing to the Rescue

Yoga breathing is great to do not just during your yoga session but anytime: in school, while you're waiting for the bus, even during TV commercials. It's especially helpful when you feel tense, angry, or tired. Several deep slow breaths can ease your tension, soothe your temper, or give you an energy boost to help you finish that nagging homework assignment. So remember, when you're mad, don't seethe – breathe!

Special Breathing Exercises

Yoga contains dozens of special breathing techniques that are fun to do and good for you. Here are just a few. Every so often, choose one of these and do it several times along with your asanas.

Humming Breath: Make a humming sound (*hmmm . . .*) as you breathe out.

Snorting Breath: Breathe in normally. Then breathe out briskly through your nose, as if you're sneezing.

Sighing Breath: Breathe in normally. Then breathe out through slightly open lips, as if you're cooling a cup of tea.

Sniffing Breath: Inhale in several short sniffs, as if you have a cold, then breathe out normally.

Darth Vader Breath: You know that throaty sound that Darth Vader makes when he breathes? You can sound like the Dark Lord too! As you breathe, tighten the muscles at the back of your throat to make a slight hissing or humming sound. Believe it or not, this is good for you! It helps you control how fast you breathe and how much air you take in, so you can use it to slow down your breath.

On to the Next Step

Now that you've warmed up and done your yoga breathing, you're ready to start moving. Bring on the asanas!

The Poses

Muscles loose from your warm-ups? Feeling nice and calm from your belly breathing? Great! Now you're ready to do some asanas.

There are dozens of poses, from simple to difficult. Following are eighteen of the most popular ones, with illustrations and instructions. But this is just a starting point. You're well advised to take a class with a certified yoga teacher and to invest in a good yoga manual. (See "Resources" on page 116.) As you do the poses, keep these guidelines in mind:

Stay Balanced

You don't have to do the postures in the order given here, but this list follows the principle of balance: forward-bending poses followed by backward-bending poses, and so on. If you change the order or substitute other postures, do so in a balanced way.

Keep Breathing

Remember to do slow even belly breathing as you do the asanas, filling and emptying your lungs as much as possible. If some parts of your body feel tight or stiff, imagine sending your breath into those tight muscles and loosening them. It really helps!

Visualizing Mind Pictures

You're sitting in class. The teacher is droning on and on. You start daydreaming. *You're riding your bike, pedaling fast through a field, tall grass rippling on either side of you, your hair streaming back in the wind . . .* Guess what – you're visualizing. That means forming a picture in your mind. Visualizing is an important part of yoga. It helps you do the poses better and get more out of them. As you do each pose, you can visualize in two ways:

1. Picture the animal or form the pose was named for.

Michael, 17: *We've got an ancient cat called Harley who's just about the laziest beast around. When he gets up from a nap – which is like all the time – he does this lo-o-o-ong lazy stretch. So when I do the Cat, I think of Harley and try to move like him.*

2. Visualize the way the pose should be done.

Anne, 13: *When I started doing yoga, I couldn't get my hips up very high in the Bridge. My teacher said to picture myself doing a perfect Bridge with my hips way up high. Yeah right, as if I'd ever get there! But you know what? I kept visualizing, and little by little, my hips started getting higher. It was like my mind was telling my body what to do.*

Suggested visualizations are given for each of the poses, but feel free to come up with your own. Whatever helps you do the pose better is a great idea!

The Poses

The Sanskrit name of each pose below is given along with the English name. For a guide to pronouncing the Sanskrit names, see the "Glossary."

Bridge – Setu Bandhasana

Setu means "bridge." As you form a bridge with your chest, hips, and legs, visualize a tall bridge arching over a rushing river.

1. Starting position: Lie on your back with your knees bent, feet flat on the floor and a hip-width apart. Stretch your arms down along your sides, palms facing down.
2. Breathe in.
3. As you breathe out, roll your hips up from the floor, starting with the tailbone, then through your middle back and upper back, until you have lifted your hips as high as you can. Keep your feet flat on the floor, and press your palms and shoulders into the floor. Make sure that your knees point forward, in line with your hips and feet.
4. Stay there for several slow breaths. Each time you breathe out, try to raise your hips a little bit higher.
5. On an out-breath, slowly roll down out of the pose, starting with your upper back, then your middle back, and finally your tailbone.

How It's Good for You

Strengthens the back. Stretches the front of the body.

Caution

If this hurts your back, roll your hips up only until your body forms a straight slanted line from your knees to your shoulders.

Knee Hug – Apanasana

This forward-bending stretch feels great after a backward-bending posture like the Bridge. As you move your knees in and out, picture the bellows of an accordion being pushed in and pulled out.

1. Starting position: Lie on your back with your legs straight.
2. Breathe in.
3. As you breathe out, bring both knees toward your chest. Cup your hands over your kneecaps.
4. As you breathe in, pull your knees away from you until your elbows straighten.
5. As you breathe out, draw your knees toward your chest, closer than before, curling your tailbone up from the floor.
6. Continue to pull your knees away and draw them in five more times, with the breath.

How It's Good for You
Stretches the lower back. Aids digestion and elimination.

Caution
Hugging your knees may create wind!

Molly, 10: *Watch out for Knee Hug if you've had chili for lunch!*

Cobra – Bhujangasana

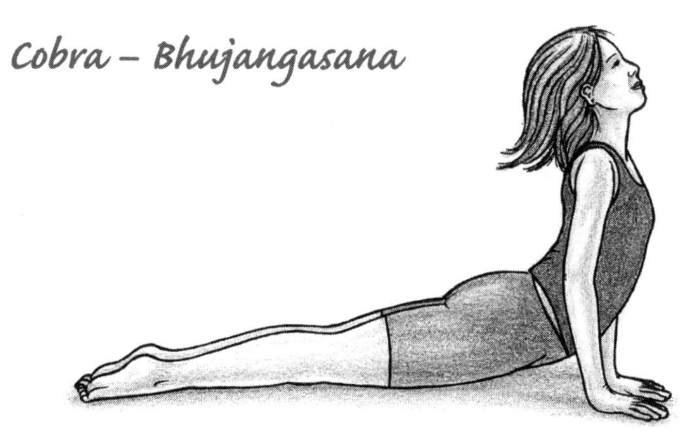

Bhujanga means "serpent." As you do this pose, pretend that you're a snake stretching slowly and gracefully toward the sky.

1. Starting position: Lie on your stomach. Bend your elbows so that your hands are flat on the floor beneath your shoulders. Keep your legs together.
2. As you breathe in, bring your head up, leading with the chin. Continue pushing up until your chest is completely off the floor and your arms are as straight as possible. Keep your elbows close to your ribs, and pull your shoulders down so your neck feels long. Look up at the ceiling.
3. Stay there for a few breaths.
4. On an out-breath, slowly lower back to the starting position.

How It's Good for You

Strengthens the back and arms. Stretches the front of the body. Opens the chest and improves posture.

Caution

If this pose hurts your lower back, do the Modified Cobra. Instead of coming up onto your hands, come up onto your forearms. Look forward and slightly up, rather than directly up at the ceiling.

Half Tortoise – Balasana

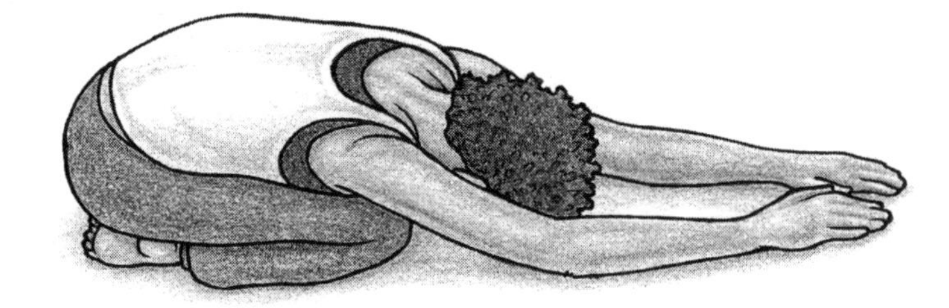

This is a variation of Child's Pose, which is described below. It's a resting posture that's good to do after a difficult or backward-bending pose like the Cobra. Imagine that the curve of your back is the rounded shell of a tortoise.

1. Starting position: Parallel hands and knees (see page 55).
2. Breathe in.
3. As you breathe out, push your hips back and sit with your bottom resting on your heels. Rest your head on the floor. Keep your arms stretched out in front of you, palms flat on the floor. Let your whole body relax.
4. Stay there for several breaths.

How It's Good for You

Stretches the arms, back, and shoulders. Massages the stomach and pelvic area.

Caution

If your knees feel uncomfortable, put a cushion under them. If they hurt, don't do this pose. Do the Cat pose instead.

Cat – Chakravakasana

Have you ever seen a cat arching and stretching after a nap? In this pose, you stre-e-e-etch like a lazy cat.

1. Starting position: Parallel hands and knees (see page 55).
2. Breathe in.
3. As you breathe out, curve your back over so it is as rounded as possible, your tailbone is tucked under, and your head is dropped down. Imagine that you are curving the front of your body over a big ball. Stay in this position for a few breaths.
4. Breathing in, arch upward, so that the top of your head and your tailbone are pointing at the ceiling and your back is dropped in a curve. Now imagine that the ball is resting on top of your back, in the curve your back is making. Try to make your waist long, and draw your shoulders away from your neck. Stay there for a few breaths.
5. Return to the starting position.

How It's Good for You

Makes the spine and pelvis more flexible. Tones the front of the body. Builds strength in the arms.

The Cat is also a great warm-up. Instead of holding in each position, keep it moving, arching upward on the in-breath and downward on the out-breath. Do eight sets (a set is one downward arch and one upward arch).

Downward Facing Dog – Adho Mukha Svanasana

Svana means "dog," *adho* means "down," and *mukha* means "face." Visualize a dog stretching as if to say, "Let's play!"

1. Starting position: Parallel hands and knees (see page 55). Tuck your toes under.
2. Breathe in.
3. As you breathe out, push your tailbone up toward the ceiling and raise your knees off the floor until your legs are straight. Try to keep your heels on the floor, although they will probably lift a little. Stretch your arms, pushing your hands into the floor, and press your chest toward your thighs. Let your head hang down between your arms. The idea is to form a triangle with your tailbone at the peak.
4. Stay there for several breaths.
5. On an out-breath, lower back to the starting position.

How It's Good for You

Stretches the backs of the legs. Strengthens the arms and wrists. Opens up the shoulders and the chest.

Holly, who has been doing yoga for four years: *When I first started doing yoga, my biggest challenge was Downward Facing Dog. It killed me at first! But gradually I got better and now I love it.*

Child's Pose – Balasana

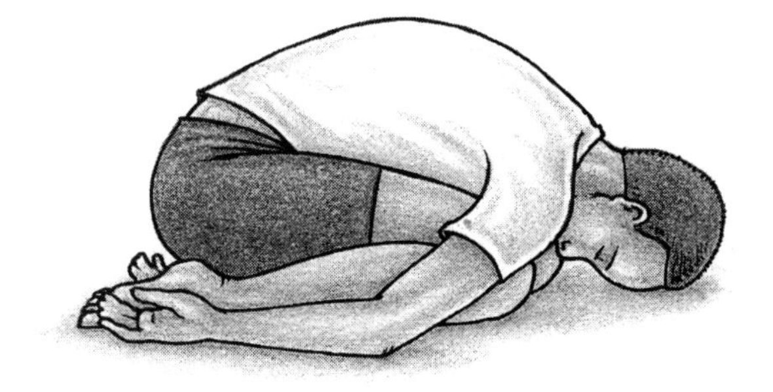

Like Half Tortoise, Child's Pose is an excellent resting posture to do after a difficult or backward-bending pose, or one that works the arms and shoulders like Downward Facing Dog. *Bala* means "child," and Balasana gets its name from the fact that some babies sleep in this position – so go back a few years and pretend that you're a snoozing baby!

1. Starting position: Parallel hands and knees (see page 55).
2. Breathe in.
3. As you breathe out, push your hips back and sit with your bottom resting on your heels. Bring your arms around to your sides with the palms facing up. Let your shoulders drop forward over your knees. Rest your forehead on the floor. Let your whole body relax.
4. Stay there for several breaths.

How It's Good for You

Stretches the lower back. Massages the stomach and pelvic area.

Caution

If you feel too much weight on your forehead, put a cushion under your head. The same goes for your knees. If your knees actually hurt, don't do this pose.

Plank – Chaturanga Dandasana

In this pose, your body is as stiff as a board – and as strong!

1. Starting position: Parallel hands and knees (see page 55).
2. Breathing in, tuck your toes under.
3. Breathing out, lift your knees and straighten your legs so that you are balanced on your palms and the balls of your feet. Make sure that your hands are directly beneath your shoulders; you may have to move your hands forward a bit. Pull in your stomach muscles. Don't arch your head; keep it in line with your back so you make a straight diagonal line from the top of your head to your heels.
4. Stay there for a few breaths, then slowly lower back to the starting position.

How It's Good for You

Strengthens the arms, shoulders, and stomach muscles. Stretches the arches.

Caution

If you find it hard to stay in this position, come onto all fours and shift your hips forward so there is more weight on your hands than on your knees.

Note: After doing the Plank, it's a good idea to do the Upper Arm Stretch (see page 53).

Pose of Eight Points – Astanga Namaskar

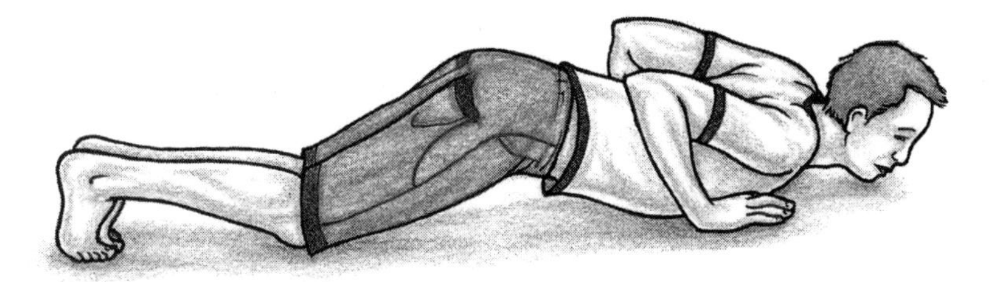

In this pose, your body makes a zigzag – your heels, your bottom, and the top of your head form the upward-pointing zigs!

1. Starting position: Lie on your stomach with your palms flat on the floor beneath your shoulders and your forehead resting on the floor.
2. Breathe in.
3. Breathing out, tuck your toes under, lift your bottom into the air, and raise your head. You should be resting on eight parts of your body: your toes, your knees, your chest, your chin, and your hands. Your knees and elbows are bent, your bottom is lifted, your back is arched, and your head is raised. As you lift your bottom, your knees will move forward slightly on the floor.
4. Stay there for a few breaths.
5. On an out-breath, untuck your toes, lower your stomach, and return to the starting position.

How It's Good for You

Stretches the stomach. Strengthens the lower back.

Caution

If this hurts your knees, put cushioning under them.

Lotus – Padmasana

Padma means "lotus," a beautiful white water flower that is a symbol of purity. When you sit in the Lotus position, imagine that your legs are the petals of the lotus, opening toward the sun.

1. Starting position: Sit with your legs stretched out in front.
2. Bend your right knee and place your right foot on your left thigh, as close to your left hip as possible.
3. Then bend your left knee and place your left foot on your right thigh, as close to your right hip as possible.
4. Rest your hands on your knees or thighs.
5. Stay there for a few breaths, then repeat on the other side.

How It's Good for You

Keeps the knees and ankles strong and flexible. Teaches you to sit correctly with the back straight.

Caution

The Lotus pose may be uncomfortable or hard to do. If so, don't force it – you could injure your joints. Try the Half Lotus (Ardha Padmasana): place one foot on the opposite thigh and keep the other leg bent in normal cross-legged position. Or use any other cross-legged or seated posture. (See "Cross-legged Comfort" on page 58.)

Note: In addition to being a pose all its own, the Lotus is often used for breathing and meditation. It is a strong stable position – once you're in it, you'll find it easy to sit up straight. If you wish, use a small pillow or folded blanket to help you sit up taller.

Seated Twist – Sukhasana

Sukha means "joy" or "pleasure," and Sukhasana is the easiest of the seated postures. This version adds a twist to spice things up. As you twist around, visualize a barber's pole with colored stripes twisting around and up, to help you sit taller and twist around farther.

1. Starting position: With your legs crossed, sit as tall and straight as you can. Pull your shoulders back and down, stack your head over your neck, and pull your chin in slightly so it is parallel with the floor. Let your hands rest on your legs.
2. Breathe in.
3. As you breathe out, twist your upper body, including your arms and head, to the right, but keep your hips facing front. Let your left hand hang over your left knee and put your right palm flat on the floor behind you. Look over your right shoulder.
4. Stay there for several breaths. With each out-breath, try to sit up taller and twist around farther.
5. Slowly come out of the twist. Cross your legs the other way and repeat the twist in the opposite direction.

How It's Good for You

Stretches the waist and neck. Strengthens the muscles of the chest, back, and shoulders.

Caution

If you find it hard to sit tall or to let your legs fall open, sit on a small pillow or folded blanket. Or do it in any other seated position. If you can, do it in the Lotus or Half Lotus position.

Mountain – Tadasana

Tada means "mountain." As you do this pose, feel as though you're as tall and broad as a mountain.

1. Starting position: Stand with your feet a hip-width apart and your arms at your sides. Make sure that your weight is evenly divided between your right foot and your left, and between your toes and your heels.
2. As you breathe in, draw your stomach muscles in and up. Pull your shoulders down, and lower your chin slightly so the back of your neck is long. Feel as though your feet are rooted to the earth, while the top of your head is pulling toward the sky.
3. Stay there for several breaths.

How It's Good for You

Improves posture. Builds strength in the back and stomach.

Note: Tadasana is the starting position for many standing postures. Here you do it with your feet a hip-width apart, but if you want to make postures more challenging, start with your feet closer together. If you want to make them easier, spread your feet wider apart.

Natalie, 15: *When I do the Mountain, I always picture Mount Fuji in Japan. It makes me feel taller and – I know this sounds corny – really majestic!*

Runner's Pose – Anjaneyasana

Imagine that you are a sprinter getting ready to run a race.

1. Starting position: Mountain pose (see page 80).
2. Breathing in, squat down and place both hands on the floor beside your feet.
3. Breathing out, reach your left leg straight back and rest on the ball of the foot, so you are lunging forward on your right leg. Make sure that your right lower leg forms a vertical line from knee to ankle, and that your right foot stays flat on the floor. Don't arch your head; keep it in line with your back so you make a straight diagonal line from the top of your head to your left heel. Keep both hands on the floor, either flat on the palms or resting on the fingertips.
4. Stay there for several breaths.
5. On an out-breath, bring your left foot forward, parallel to your right foot and a hip-width apart. Roll up into Mountain pose. Repeat on the other side.

How It's Good for You

Stretches the hamstrings (the long muscles at the back of the legs) and the front of the hips. Strengthens the arms, back, and shoulders.

Caution

If you find it hard to keep your back leg straight, bend it and let your knee and lower leg rest on the floor. Don't put too much weight on your knee; keep more weight on your front foot.

Triangle – Utthita Trikonasana

In this pose, you're making two triangles with your body: a larger one formed by your legs and the floor, and a smaller one formed by your lower arm, the side of your chest, and your leg.

1. Starting position: Mountain pose (see page 80).
2. Breathe in.
3. As you breathe out, step sideways with your right foot to bring your legs wide apart, toes pointing front. Keep your weight evenly balanced. Bring your arms out to the sides at shoulder level, palms facing down. Stay there for a breath or two.
4. On an in-breath, turn out your right foot so that the toes are pointing to the side, and look to the right. Turn your left foot in slightly. Breathe out.
5. Breathe in.
6. As you breathe out, shift your hips to the left, and start tilting your whole upper body sideways over your right leg. As your chest leans to the side, reach your right hand toward your right foot and your left hand toward the ceiling. Place your right hand on your thigh, your shin, your ankle, your foot, or the floor. Look up at your left hand.
7. Stay there for several breaths. With each breath, push a little farther into your left hip, reach a little higher with your left hand, and lean a little farther over your right leg. Keep your body facing front. Try to feel as if both shoulders are pushing against an imaginary wall.
8. To come out of the position, breathe out, bend your right knee slightly, push away, and come upright. Turn your right foot forward, bring your feet together, and lower your arms.
9. Repeat on the left side.

How It's Good for You

Stretches the hips. Strengthens the legs and the muscles in the chest.

Caution

If you can't reach your lower leg or ankle, place a block or thick book behind your foot and rest your hand on it. You may also bend the knee of the turned-out leg if you need to.

Variation: Twisted Triangle – Parivritta Trikonasana

Parivritta means "twisted" or "revolved." Picture a square piece of paper being folded in half diagonally. That's what you're trying to do with your left hand and your right foot.

1. Get into Triangle pose on the right side.
2. Breathe in.
3. As you breathe out, twist your upper body to face back wards, across your right leg. Place your left hand on your right leg or ankle or on the floor in front of you, wherever it can comfortably reach.
4. Lift your right arm straight up behind you and look at it.
5. Stay there for a few breaths, then untwist and come back up straight, facing front. Turn your right foot forward, bring your feet together, and lower your arms.
6. Repeat on the left side.

How It's Good for You

Stretches the waist and leg muscles. Strengthens the lower back.

Cautions

If you feel discomfort in your lower back, twist less, place your lower hand higher up on your leg, or use a block to rest your hand on.

Standing Backbend – Prstha Vakrasana

Time for a tummy stretch! As you do this posture, imagine that you are arching backward over a big curved rainbow.

1. Starting position: Mountain pose (see page 80).
2. Bring your hands together at the middle of your chest, level with your heart, palms touching. Let your elbows fall. Keep your shoulders down; don't let them creep up toward your ears. This is called the Prayer Position.
3. Breathing in, stretch your arms up over your head, and arch backward. Look up and back. You may keep your palms together or let them open slightly, but keep your arms level with your ears. Press your hips forward. Think of lifting up and over a rounded shape, rather than bending straight back.
4. This is an intense stretch, so stay there for just a breath or two.
5. On an out-breath, return to the starting position.

How It's Good for You

Stretches the whole front of your body, especially the hips. Strengthens the lower back.

Caution

Stretch only as far back as is comfortable. Be careful not to strain your back.

Standing Forward Bend – Uttanasana

Ut means "intensity," and *tan* is "to stretch." As you do Uttanasana, think of your tailbone pointing straight up to the ceiling. That will help you bend over farther.

1. Starting position: Mountain pose (see page 80).
2. Breathe in.
3. As you breathe out, press your hips slightly back, and lean forward with your upper body, including your arms. Bend over as far as you can, bringing your chest toward your thighs. Keep your weight even on your feet and your knees slightly bent. Let your head and arms hang down loosely. If you are very flexible, you might even be able to rest your palms on the floor.

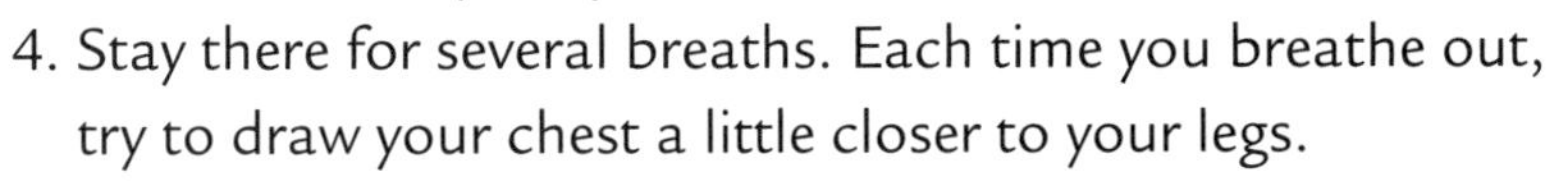

4. Stay there for several breaths. Each time you breathe out, try to draw your chest a little closer to your legs.
5. On an in-breath, roll back up to the starting position.

How It's Good for You

Stretches the hamstrings. Lengthens the spine.

Caution

Bend over only as far as is comfortable. If your back is stiff or your legs are very tight, you may want to put blocks on the floor in front of your feet and rest your hands on them.

Esta, who has been doing yoga since the age of 12: *One of my favorite poses is Standing Forward Bend. I find it relaxing, and it's easy for me to go deep inside myself in that position.*

Tree – Vrksasana

What's your favorite tree? In this pose, you're that tree – tall, broad, and balanced. Imagine that your standing leg and foot are the roots, anchoring you to the earth, and that your upper body is the branches and leaves, reaching toward the sun.

1. Starting position: Mountain pose (see page 80).
2. Breathe in and shift your weight to your left leg.
3. As you breathe out, lift your right foot, bending your right knee out to the side. Pick up your right ankle with your right hand. Place the bottom of your right foot on the inside of your left thigh, as high up as possible. Press your right knee slightly back. Pull up on your left leg so you feel tall and stretched, but keep your foot flat on the floor.
4. Bring your hands into Prayer Position (see step 2 of "Standing Backbend," page 84).
5. Stay there for several breaths. To help you concentrate, find a spot to focus on. If you feel very balanced, bring your hands up over your head, arms straight and palms still touching. Move slowly so you don't wreck your balance!
6. If you wobble or have to put your foot down, that's okay. Slowly go back into the pose.
7. On an out-breath, slowly return to the starting position.
8. Repeat on the left side.

How It's Good for You

Improves your balance and concentration. Increases the flexibility of your hips.

Sun Salutation – Surya Namaskar

This is a series of twelve postures – all of which you now know – that you do in a continuous sequence. It's a way of greeting the sun and saying thanks for the energy it gives.

Because the Sun Salutation is made up of forward-bending and backward-bending poses that follow one another in turn, it's a perfect balance of stretches for the front and back of your body. The continuous movement gives you a workout too. You can do the Sun Salutation as a warm-up or as a regular pose.

Each movement of the Sun Salutation is designed to be done on one in-breath or out-breath. For example, you do the Cobra on one in-breath and then move into Downward Facing Dog on the next out-breath. Try to make one part flow into the next, so that the whole series becomes one fluid continuous movement. When you are first learning the steps, your movements may be a little jerky, but once you know the series you will be able to do it smoothly and continuously. The whole sequence takes about a half-minute for each side.

As you do the Sun Salutation, think about greeting the sun, and feel its energy coursing through your body.

1. Mountain pose *Tadasana*
   Stand with your feet a hip-width apart. Bring your hands together in Prayer Position (see pages 80 and 84).
2. Standing Backbend *Prstha Vakrasana*
   Breathing in, stretch your arms up over your head and arch into Standing Backbend (see page 84).
3. Standing Forward Bend *Uttanasana*
   Breathing out, come back to an upright position, arms over your head, then stretch forward and down into Standing Forward Bend (see page 85).
4. Runner's Pose *Anjaneyasana*
   Breathing in, squat down and stretch your left leg back into Runner's Pose (see page 81), so you are lunging forward on your right leg.
5. Plank *Chaturanga Dandasana*
   Hold your breath (you have just inhaled on the Runner's Pose). Reach your right leg back to meet the left and go into the Plank (see page 76).
6. Pose of Eight Points *Astanga Namaskar*
   Breathing out, slowly lower your body into the Pose of Eight Points (see page 77).
7. Cobra *Bhujangasana*
   Breathing in, untuck your toes, lower your legs and hips, and push up into the Cobra (see page 71).
8. Downward Facing Dog *Adho Mukha Svanasana*
   Breathing out, tuck your toes under and push back into Downward Facing Dog (see page 74).
9. Runner's Pose *Anjaneyasana*
   Breathing in, bring your left foot forward into Runner's Pose on your left leg (see page 81 and step 4 above).
10. Standing Forward Bend *Uttanasana*
    Breathing out, bring your right foot forward, parallel to

your left foot and a hip-width apart. Bend over in Standing Forward Bend (see page 85 and step 3 above).

11. Standing Backbend *Prstha Vakrasana*
    Breathing in, roll up to standing, bring your arms up over your head, and arch backward (see page 84 and step 2 above).
12. Mountain *Tadasana*
    Breathing out, return to the Mountain with your hands in Prayer Position.
13. Repeat the entire sequence, this time lunging first on the left leg.

How It's Good for You

Stretches and tones the whole body. Gets your breathing going and warms you up.

> **Lucky Sun**
>
> The Hindu Sun god, Surya, has traditionally been shown as a red man with three eyes and four arms, riding in a chariot drawn by seven mares. He is thought to be a kind god who can heal sick people. Even today in India, people place the Sun symbol over shops because they believe it will bring good fortune.

On to the Next Step

Wow! You've worked hard. Now you're ready for the final stage of your yoga session: relaxation.

Rela-a-a-ax!

Congratulations! You've warmed up, done your breathing, and worked your way through a series of postures. Now it's time to reward yourself with a soothing relaxation session.

Relaxation isn't just about resting tired muscles. It's also about restoring your energy and bringing yourself to a deeper state of calmness after the concentration and effort of the poses. It gets you ready to face the world again, refreshed and renewed.

Finish each yoga session with several minutes of relaxation. You may do this lying down in the Corpse pose (see next page) or sitting in a comfortable position.

Keep in mind that once you stop doing the poses, you may cool down quickly. To avoid getting chilled, cover yourself with a light blanket or put on extra clothing.

Relax Around the Clock

Relaxation exercises are great to do any time you need a lift:

- after school, to give you energy for sports or other activities
- before bed, to help you sleep soundly
- when you're sick (you can do them in bed or sitting in a chair)
- whenever you feel tense, angry, or distressed

Corpse Pose – Savasana

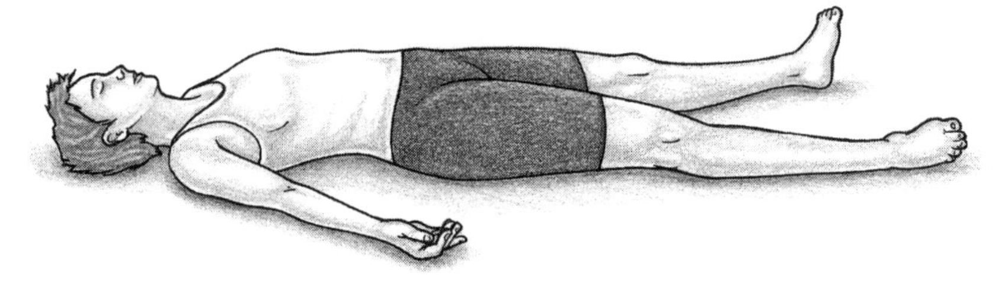

No, you don't have to be dead to do the Corpse pose! This is the classic position for yoga relaxation. As you do the Corpse, imagine that you can float above your body and look down at yourself. See yourself in a state of complete rest, with every muscle relaxed. Aahhh . . . doesn't that feel good?

1. Lie on your back with your legs stretched out and slightly apart, and your arms comfortably at your sides, palms facing up. You may want to put a rolled-up towel under your knees; this will help your lower back press gently into the floor. Close your eyes.
2. Mentally check your whole body, from your toes to the top of your head. Note any stress, tension, or fatigue. Take a few deep breaths, and as you breathe out, let your stress and tension float out and away.
3. Breathe slowly and smoothly. Do belly breathing, but instead of pushing your breath out, just let it flow out easily; don't worry about emptying your lungs. If you wish, choose one of the relaxation exercises from the list below. If not, simply breathe and try to let every muscle relax and melt into the floor.
4. Come out of your relaxation slowly and gently. Don't get up too fast – if you do, you may get dizzy. Open your eyes, roll onto your side, and sit up. Then stand up slowly.

How It's Good for You
Relaxes tight or tired muscles. Restores energy and refreshes you.

Caution
The only danger in doing the Corpse pose is that you might fall asleep!

Holly, who has been doing yoga for four years: *My favorite poses are the Corpse, Half Tortoise, and Child's Pose. Are you beginning to see a pattern here?*

Relaxation Exercises

Try some of these relaxation techniques and see which ones you like. Most of them work best in the Corpse position, although you can also do them sitting.

Tense and Release: Tighten the muscles in your feet. Really clench them. Hold for a few seconds, then let go. Feel your feet relax. Do the same in turn with your legs, buttocks, stomach, arms, shoulders (pull them up toward your ears), neck (tuck your chin way in), and face. Finally, tense your entire body, then let go. By now, you should be relaxed from head to toe!

Floating on a Cloud: Imagine that a fluffy white cloud floats out of the sky, down toward you. It rests beside you. Your body floats up and onto the cloud. It's as soft as the softest bed. The cloud slowly lifts off the ground and rises into the sky. It floats for a while, then slowly comes back down. Your body floats off, feeling totally weightless.

In and Out: Concentrate on your breath. As you breathe in, imagine that all the good things you want, like happiness and peace, are flowing into your body along with the breath. As you breathe out, imagine that all the bad things, like tension and violence, are flowing out.

Beach Bunny: Imagine that you're sunbathing on a warm sandy beach. (Of course, you've got your sunscreen on!) A gentle breeze is blowing and waves are lapping at the shore. Feel the sun soak into your skin, warming and relaxing every part of your body.

Bathing Beauty: If you like to take baths, this is a great exercise for you. Imagine that you're getting into a nice warm bath. Maybe you've put in some scented bath beads, and the fragrance floats up. Slip your feet into the water, then your legs, your middle, and your back all the way up to your neck. Rest your head against the back of the tub. Let your arms and legs float. Aahhh!

Colors: What's your favorite color? As you breathe in, imagine a wave of that beautiful color streaming into your body, filling every space. As you breathe out, imagine that all the dull dirty gray inside you is floating out.

Rainbow Countdown: Make your mind blank, like a dark TV screen. Now picture a red number 7 in your mind's eye. Hold it there for a moment, then let it float away, out of sight. Do the same with an orange 6, a yellow 5, a green 4, a blue 3, an indigo (blue-purple) 2, and a purple 1. After the 1 has gone, let your mind be empty again.

Bird Feeder: Imagine that you are lying in a grassy meadow with birds flying all around. In your upturned hands there is bird seed.

You must lie perfectly still so that the birds will come and eat from your hands.

Your Choice: What images or feelings help you relax? As you do your relaxation, you will discover your own exercises. Have fun with them!

Try This

You know how noodles are stiff and hard when they are dry, but turn soft and limp once they are cooked? Take the "noodle test" to see if you are "cooked"! While you are relaxing, get a friend to lift your arms and legs off the floor. Are your "noodles" done?

Meditation

Meditation is a way of stilling the mind. It's very similar to relaxation, but it goes deeper. Whereas relaxation's goal is to rest the body and mind, meditation is designed to bring you to an inner place of concentration and stillness.

For some people, meditation has a spiritual side. They meditate to reach a state of union with God or the divine spirit or the universe. You may or may not be interested in that purpose. Either way, meditation can be a valuable addition to your yoga practice, bringing you a deep sense of peace and calmness.

Why meditate? Because it makes you feel good, that's why! If you have a busy stressful life, meditation can help you manage your stress – and that can improve your health and sense of well-being. People who meditate say that it makes them feel more alert and alive.

There are physical benefits too. In addition to helping you feel more relaxed, meditation slows your breathing and lowers your blood pressure. It also boosts your immune system, so you are better able to fight disease and infection.

Did You Know?

Laboratory tests have shown that a person's brain waves are slower and smoother during meditation than during sleep!

How to Meditate

Here are a couple of tips to help you meditate successfully:

- Choose a time and place. You can meditate anywhere, anytime, but it's best to do it at the same time of day and in the same place. Naturally, you'll want to choose a quiet space where you won't be interrupted.
- Choose a posture that works for you – sitting on the floor or in a chair, or lying down. Whichever position you choose, keep your body straight and aligned but relaxed.

To begin your meditation session, get comfortable in the meditation position you have chosen. Close your eyes. Try to let your mind be empty. If you wish, use one of the techniques from the list below. If not, sit quietly and breathe. If your mind wanders, don't get discouraged or mad at yourself. Simply let go of the distracting thought and return to your focus and your stillness. If you're a beginner, add five to ten minutes of meditation to the end of your yoga session. As you get better, you can lengthen the time.

Meditation Techniques

Meditation is like growing: you can't *make* it happen, you just have to *let* it happen. Still, there are techniques that can help you concentrate. Here are suggestions:

- Repeat a sound or phrase to yourself, either silently or aloud. For example, you might say "peace" or "Om" (a mystical sound thought to contain all the sounds of the universe). Or you might repeat an affirmation (a positive statement) such as "I am at peace" or "I am still." Chanting a word or phrase over and over is called mantra yoga.
- Visualize a picture. It could be your image of God, a natural form such as a flower, or your favorite color. Hold it in your mind's eye.
- With your eyes either fully or partly open, gaze at something. Keep staring at it.
- Focus on your breath. Without changing it or doing yoga breathing, simply observe it as it comes in and goes out.

When you finish your meditation, open your eyes. Gently stretch. If you are lying down, roll to your side and sit up. Take a deep breath and stand up slowly. Now . . . don't you feel great?

After reading through the last few chapters, some of you may be thinking, "That sounds great! When can I start?" Others may be thinking, "There's no way I can do all that. I'm too stiff. (Or I'm in a wheelchair.) (Or I have no sense of balance.) I might as well not bother."

If you're in the second group, don't despair. You *can* do yoga, no matter what your limitations. The trick is to make it work for *you*, to find the level where you *can* do the technique and go from there. Even if all you can do are the breathing exercises, that's better than nothing, and you'll get some benefit from that much practice.

Here are some tips for adapting yoga for *you*.

If You Have Disabilities

If you have a physical impairment and you're thinking that yoga isn't for you, think again. Yoga is an excellent form of exercise for people whose physical movement is limited.

Of course, yoga isn't a magic pill; it can't restore function to a disabled part of your body. But if you stretch, breathe, and do the asanas to whatever extent you can, you can improve the flexi-

bility and health of the rest of your body, and that can help overcome problems caused by your disability.

Consult a yoga teacher or physiotherapist for help in adapting the yoga postures for you. Also, see "Resources" (page 116) for information for people with special needs. Meanwhile, here are a few suggestions:

Breathe, Breathe, Breathe!: Do belly breathing (see the chapter "Brea-a-a-athe!"), breathing in and out as slowly and fully as possible. This is really helpful, especially if your movement is limited. Also, try some of the special breathing techniques in the chapter on breathing.

Warming Up: Do the warm-ups in the chapter "Getting Warmed Up." Most can be done either standing or sitting.

Stretch: If you can't stand up to stretch, try the lying-down version below. If you're in a wheelchair, try the wheelchair exercise.

Lying-Down Stretch

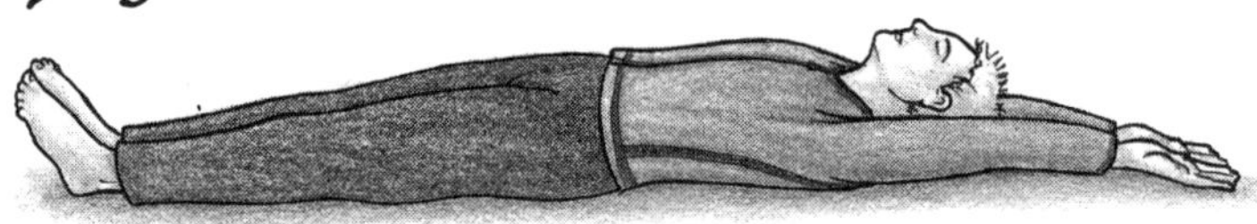

1. Starting position: Lie on your back with your feet together and your arms by your sides, palms down.
2. As you breathe in, lift your arms up in front of you and, tracing a big half-circle in the air, stretch them over your head until the backs of your hands touch the floor behind your head.

3. Imagine that someone is pulling your toes and someone else is pulling your hands, and stre-e-etch!
4. Breathing out, bring your arms up, trace another big half-circle, and return to the starting position.
5. Repeat several times.

Wheelchair Exercise

1. Starting position: Sit up as straight as you can.
2. As you breathe in, swing your arms out to the sides and up over your head, lifting your upper body as high as possible.
3. As you breathe out, stretch your arms forward and down, and lean over so that your chest rests on your legs. Let your head fall forward. Stay there for several slow breaths.
4. Breathing in, slowly sit up and bring your arms forward and back up over your head.
5. Breathing out, lower your arms to your sides.
6. Repeat several times.

Go At Your Own Pace

Looking at pictures in a yoga manual can be inspiring – and also discouraging. The people in the photographs are so darn good! When they bend over in Standing Forward Bend, their palms rest flat on the floor and their chests are touching their knees. When they push up into the Cobra, their arms are straight. When they do the Bridge, they get their hips up so high, you could drive a freight train underneath! How is an ordinary mortal to compete with that kind of perfection?

Aha! There's that word – "compete." The whole point of yoga is *not* to compete. Whether you are looking at the other people in your class or at pictures in a book, remember that no one else's progress matters except your own. Everyone, no matter how advanced, has room for improvement, and every true yogi is working to improve all the time.

Keep in mind that everyone has different physical abilities. If you need to rest your hands on a block in Standing Forward Bend and the person in the picture doesn't, that's fine. If you can get your heels flat on the floor in Downward Facing Dog and the person next to you in class can't, that's fine too.

So go at your own pace. It's *your* breath, *your* body – *your* yoga practice. And remember to follow these important guidelines:

- Don't push to the point of pain. If a pose hurts, don't do it, or do it at a simpler level. No matter what, don't force yourself to do something painful just because everyone else is doing it, or to prove that you can.
- Use props if you need them. It's better to do a pose correctly *with* assistance than to do it incorrectly *without*.
- If you have a medical problem, check with your doctor before starting to do yoga.
- When you're sick, don't do yoga. When you get better, start again gradually.
- Be very careful with inverted postures such as Shoulder Stand, Head Stand, and Plow. They can put pressure on your head, neck, and spine. Make sure you know how to do them properly before you attempt them.
- Follow the principle of balance so that you work all parts of your body and don't strain any parts by overusing them.
- Keep breathing! The breath is truly powerful. Often, when you're stiff, or when you feel stuck at a certain point in a pose, yoga breathing can help you get past the point of stiffness and onto a new level of flexibility and ease.

Remember, too, that yoga can change your physical abilities, if you do it long enough. You may start as a person who can't sit in the Lotus pose and become a person who can. You may morph from someone with horrible balance to someone who can nail the Tree every time. And if that happens, you're in a great position to pass on a precious gift to other beginners – encouragement. Just imagine this scenario:

A new student – let's say it's a guy – joins your class. The class is doing the Triangle. Out of the corner of your eye, you can see that he's not very far over to the side, and you can hear his sighs of discouragement. "That was pathetic," you hear him say under his breath as the pose comes to an end.

After class you go over to the new guy. "Hey, don't worry," you say with a smile. "When I was starting out, I mangled the Triangle. I could only get my hand on my knee, and I could only stay in the position for about ten seconds."

The new guy looks at you incredulously. "You?" he breathes. "But you're so . . . *good*!"

"Yeah," you say with a grin, "and you will be, too!"

Making Yoga Part of Your Life

It's one thing to read about yoga in a book, or even try it once or twice. It's another thing to make it part of your life. How do you fit a yoga practice into your busy schedule? How do you keep from getting bored with the same old exercises? How do you stay motivated, so that you continue to practice and improve? If these questions are running through your mind, stay tuned – this chapter answers them.

Planning Your Routine

The asanas in the chapter "The Poses" make up just one possible yoga routine. But there are so many postures to choose from! With ideas from a yoga class or a yoga manual, you can design your own routine, and vary it every day to keep it fun and interesting.

Here are two sample yoga programs: a "quickie" for days when you are rushed, and a complete one for days when you have more time. Each routine carefully combines a variety of poses to give your body a balanced workout.

You already know some of the poses in the sample routines below, but others will be new to you, and some of those are more

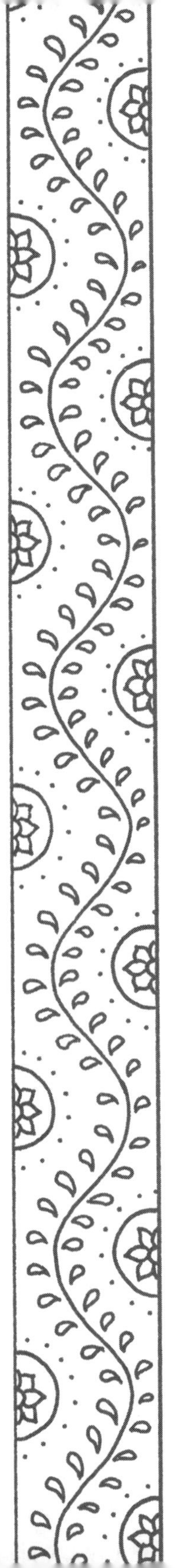

advanced. Short descriptions are given for the new poses, but they are far from complete. Before trying any new poses, be sure to consult a yoga teacher or a good yoga manual for complete instructions to make sure that you do them correctly. And – as always – don't do anything that hurts or that strains your body.

Routine 1

Too busy to do a complete yoga session? This mini-routine will do in a pinch. Because the Sun Salutation does such a good job of stretching the front and back of your body, all you need to do is add a side stretch and a twist, and you've worked your whole body. This routine will take 10 to 15 minutes. (Note: Although it's always a good idea to warm up before starting yoga, you can skip the usual warm-ups because the Sun Salutation serves as a warm-up here.)

1. Breathing (see chapter "Brea-a-a-athe").
2. Sun Salutation *Surya Namaskar* (see page 87).
   Do this at least twice on each side, four times in total.
3. Triangle *Utthita Trikonasana* (see page 82).
4. Twisted Triangle *Parivritta Trikonasana* (see page 83).
5. Relaxation (see chapter "Rela-a-a-ax!").

Routine 2

This session will take about a half-hour to complete.

1. Warm-ups (see chapter "Getting Warmed Up").
2. Breathing (see chapter "Brea-a-a-athe").
3. Bow *Dhanurasana*
   Zing! In this pose, you form an archer's bow with your body. Lie on your stomach, grab your ankles behind you, and pull upward. Your arms are the string, and the whole front of your body is the curved wooden bow.
4. Knee-to-Chest Pose *Apanasana*

In this pose, lying on your back, you pull one knee toward your chest while keeping the other leg straight on the floor with the foot flexed. This asana is great for stretching the backs of your legs, your buttocks, and your lower back.

5. Seated Twist *Sukhasana* (see page 79).
6. Half Moon *Ardha Chandrasana*

   In this pose, you trace a crescent moon with your body. Standing with your feet together and your arms overhead, palms touching, lean sideways into one hip and let your head and hands curve in the opposite direction. Come back upright, then lean the other way. Do you feel the stretch in your hip?
7. Warrior III *Virabhadrasana*

   In this pose, you balance on one foot, leaning forward with your arms extended in front of you and the other leg lifted behind you. The idea is to form a T with your body: your standing leg is the vertical line, and the rest of your body, from your hands to your back foot, is the crossbar. How long can you stay up?
8. Downward Facing Dog *Adho Mukha Svanasana* (see page 74).
9. Relaxation (see chapter "Rela-a-a-ax!").

Making Up Your Own

Now it's your turn. Grab a piece of paper. Using the postures listed above, or from other sources, plan your own routine. Include as many different kinds of poses as you can so you work your whole body.

The columns below can help you. Choose one of the five main positions from the list on the left and combine it with one of the types of movement from the list on the right. Mix and match as many different combinations as you can.

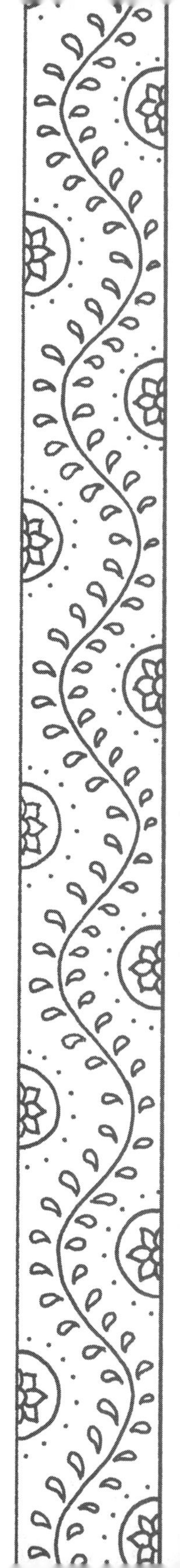

Positions	***Movements***
Seated	Forward-bending
Standing	Backward-bending
Supine	Twisting
Prone	Sideways-bending
Inverted	

For example, Knee-to-Chest Pose is a supine pose with a forward bend. The Bow combines prone and backward-bending movements. If you put together “standing” and “sideways bending,” you could do Triangle or Half Moon.

Need more ideas? This chart tells you the position and the type of movement for every pose mentioned in this book.

Pose	**Position**	**Movement**
Bow *Dhanurasana*	Prone	Backward-bending
Bridge *Setu Bandhasana*	Supine	Backward-bending
Cat *Chakravakasana*	Prone	Forward- and backward-bending
Child’s Pose *Balasana*	Prone	Forward-bending
Cobra *Bhujangasana*	Prone	Backward-bending
Downward Facing Dog *Adho Mukha Svanasana*	Prone, Inverted	Forward-bending

Pose	Position	Movement
Half Lotus *Ardha Padmasana*	Seated	
Half Moon *Ardha Chandrasana*	Standing	Sideways-bending
Half Tortoise *Balasana*	Prone	Forward-bending
Knee Hug *Apanasana*	Supine	Forward-bending
Knee-to-Chest Pose *Apanasana*	Supine	Forward-bending
Lotus *Padmasana*	Seated	
Mountain *Tadasana*	Standing	
Plank *Chaturanga Dandasana*	Prone, Balancing	
Pose of Eight Points *Astanga Namaskar*	Prone	Backward-bending
Runner's Pose *Anjaneyasana*	Prone	Forward-bending

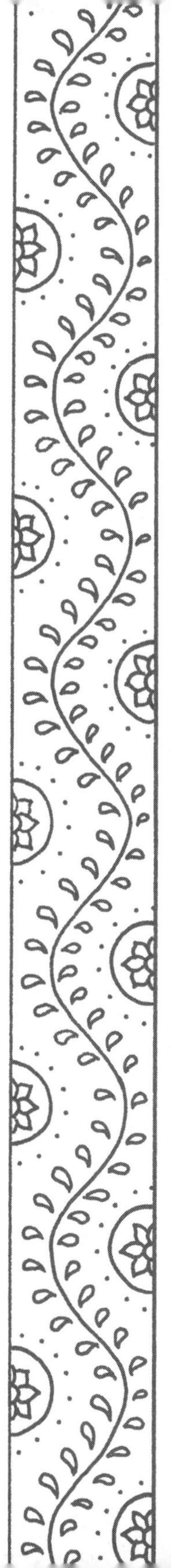

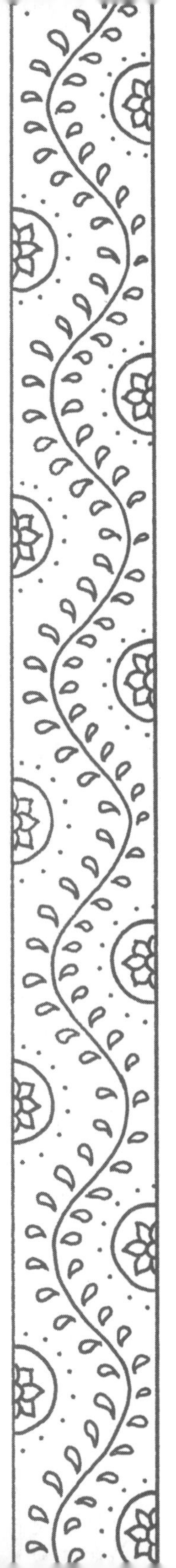

Pose	Position	Movement
Seated Twist *Sukhasana*	Seated	Twisting
Standing Backbend *Prstha Vakrasana*	Standing	Backward-bending
Standing Forward Bend *Uttanasana*	Standing	Forward-bending
Sun Salutation *Surya Namaskar*	Standing, Prone, Inverted	Forward- and backward-bending
Tree *Vrksasana*	Standing,	Balancing
Triangle *Utthita Trikonasana*	Standing	Sideways-bending
Twisted Triangle *Parivritta Trikonasana*	Standing and twisting	Sideways-bending
Warrior III *Virabhadrasana*	Standing, Balancing	Forward-bending

As you plan your routine, follow the principle of balance, and always do a backward-bending pose after a forward-bending pose, and so on.

It may be difficult to fit all of the positions and types of movement into one routine. Just make sure you cover them over a few days' worth of yoga routines.

Have fun – and happy stretching!

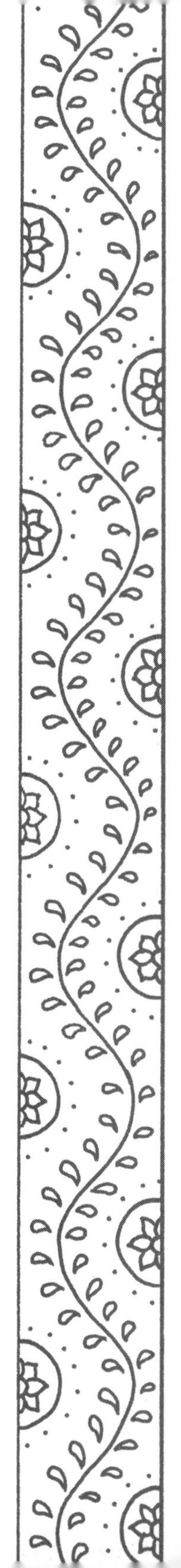

Finding Time for Yoga

Okay, you've read about how great yoga is, you've bought a mat, and you can't wait to start. But between school and soccer practice, music lessons and household chores, outings with friends and maybe even a part-time job, how on earth are you going to fit it into your life?

The answer: whenever and however you can. Probably the easiest way to get going and stick with it is to take a class. Many people find that if they have a scheduled class to go to, they'll do their yoga regularly – and if they don't, they won't. Here are some other ways to fit yoga in:

- If you're an early riser, you might be able to do a short session before school.
- Do it when you get home from school (*before* you flop down in front of the TV!) or before bed.
- If the week is just too hectic, set aside time on the weekends.
- See if you can get your friends interested, and form a yoga club. You can keep each other motivated, give each other support, and take turns leading the group in your favorite posture. Besides, it's fun to do yoga with others!
- Give up a half-hour of TV or computer time and do yoga instead.

You can even find ways to cram little bits of yoga into odd moments:

- When you're waiting for the bus or in a store lineup, practice the Mountain pose.
- Do some deep breathing when you're sitting in the dentist's chair.
- During study breaks, do a few of your favorite stretches.
- During commercials, tune out the TV and tune in some yoga poses.

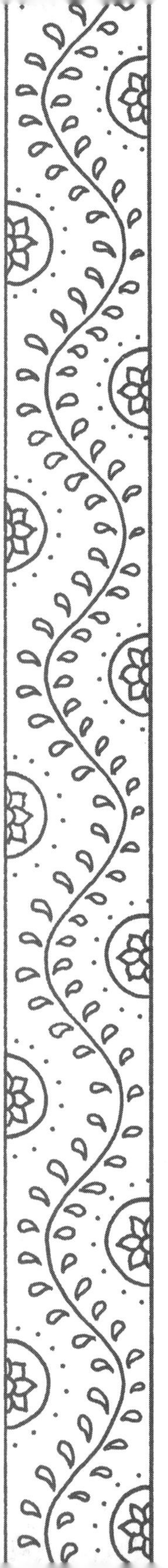

Although it may take a little juggling to make room for yoga in your busy life, you'll find it's worth it. But if you miss a yoga session or find that you have to cut your sessions short, don't get mad at yourself. A little yoga is better than none.

Keeping Up Your Motivation

Yoga is one of those practices that has a built-in reward system. The more you do it, the better you get. And the better you get, the more you want to do it. But, like everyone else, you're only human; once the initial excitement wears off, it's natural to slack off a little. So how do you keep yourself motivated? Keep track of your progress. And reward yourself!

Keep Track of Your Progress

Keeping a record of your yoga practice is a good idea for several reasons. Reason number one: it helps you remember what poses you've done – it's hard to keep all that information in your head. Reason number two: it's a place to set goals and note what poses you want to try or how you want to challenge yourself. Reason number three: it's a way to keep track of any problems you're having, so you'll remember to work on them. Reason number four, and the most important: it provides a way to see how far you've come – so you can feel good about yourself!

Each day, write down what poses you've done and any notes or comments you want to remember. Here are examples of what other kids have written:

Ryan, 12: *Nearly got my heels down in DF Dog! Yay!*

Anne, 13: *Bit of discomfort in Cobra. Remember to reach forward, not scrunch back.*

Michael, 17: *Balance good on left leg in Tree but right leg sucked. Maybe twisting a bit? Keep hips forward.*

Natalie, 15: *Got fingertips on floor in Forward Bend! I'm amazing!*

Where should you write down this information? Anywhere that's convenient.

- Buy a notebook and make it your yoga journal.
- Use that unused diary that Aunt Hortense gave you for your last birthday.
- Write it on a calendar.
- Some yoga books have blank pages for making notes and recording progress.
- Create a computer file that's just for your yoga notes.

Reward Yourself

You might be the kind of person that finds that reading back over your yoga journal and seeing how far you've come is reward enough. Then again, you might not. If you're the second type (and most of us are), go ahead and reward yourself when you reach certain milestones.

What type of milestones? Any that matter to you. For example, your milestones might be

- when you've been doing yoga for a certain period of time – say, a month
- when you've met your goal of doing yoga three times a week, or for 20 minutes each time
- when you've reached a certain level of performance – for instance, getting your hand on your ankle in the Triangle or staying up longer in the Tree
- when you've tried a new posture
- when you've mastered a challenging pose

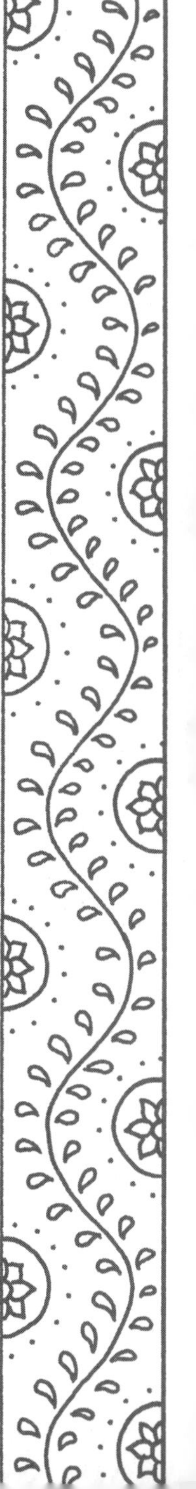

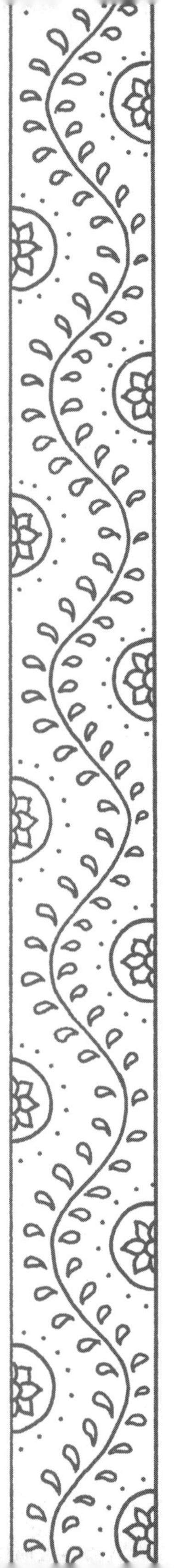

When you reach that goal, be sure to congratulate yourself in fine fashion. You might

- tell your family or friends
- buy yourself a little treat
- draw a star in your yoga journal
- give yourself a few extra minutes of relaxation
- look in the mirror and say, "Way to go!"

Hey, don't be shy. You deserve it!

Making the Commitment

Enough talk. Now it's time to get off your you-know-what and actually do it. Make that phone call to the local rec center. Put on your shorts and start stretching. Take a class. Borrow a yoga book from the library. Talk to your friends. Query your gym teacher. Start visualizing cats and dogs.

Yoga may turn out to be one of those things that you try briefly and then discard. On the other hand, it may be one of those things that, the very first time you do it, makes you say, "Wow! This is for me!" You never know. And there's only one way to find out.

So go for it. You'll probably be stiff at first. Maybe a little uncoordinated. Your mind might wander. Your balance might be wobbly. You might get discouraged. You might feel like quitting.

Don't. Hang in there. Give yourself a month or two. You may find that, after a rough start, things start to change . . .

One day, stretching up in the Cobra, you'll feel the whole front of your body expanding like a rubber band, long . . . longer . . . and it feels great! Bending over in Standing Forward Bend, you'll find your fingers inching toward your ankles . . . your toes . . . the floor! Coming out of your relaxation at the end of class, you'll realize that, although you felt tired and cranky going in, you now feel like you could run a marathon! And you can't wait for your next yoga session.

Guess what. You're hooked. Just like millions of kids all over the world. Kids who have fun pretending to be bridges and trees. Kids who dig feeling stretched and strong. Kids who love the peaceful place yoga puts them in.

Kids like Molly and Michael. We'll let them have the last word:

Molly, 10: *Yoga is so much fun. My friends and I laugh when we fall over, and we really get into being animals and things. I know it's good for me and all that, but I do it because it makes me happy!*

Michael, 17: *I started doing yoga because I thought it would make me a better football player – and it has. I'm definitely looser and more alert on the field. But I've stayed with it for a different reason. I don't quite know how to put this, but yoga helps me be myself. I'm in my own space, in my own head. I'm not competing or performing, I'm just letting the movement and the breathing take me inside. And when I come out, I feel totally great.*

Books

Children's Book of Yoga: Games and Exercises Mimic Plants and Animals and Objects by Thia Luby. Santa Fe, New Mexico: Clear Light Publishers, 1998. Shows children how yoga postures were derived.

The Complete Idiot's Guide to Yoga With Kids by Jodi Komitor and Eve Adamson. Alpha Books, 2000. Instructions for how to get kids of all ages started in yoga.

The Complete Illustrated Guide to Yoga by Howard Kent. Shaftesbury, Dorset: Element Books Limited, 1999. For adults, but with good illustrations that kids can follow.

K.I.S.S. Guide to Yoga by Shakta Kaur Khalsa. London: Dorling Kindersley, 2001. For adults, but simple enough for kids to use.

Yoga for Children: A Complete Illustrated Guide to Yoga by Swati Chanchani and Rajiv Chanchani. New Delhi: UBS Publishers' Distributors Ltd., 2000. Comprehensive guide from a traditional Indian perspective.

Yoga for Children by Stella Weller. London: Thorsons (an imprint of Harper Collins Publishers), 1996. Complete and easy to follow.

Yoga for the Special Child by Sonia Sumar. Buckingham, Virginia: Special Yoga Publications, 1996. Adapted postures and breathing exercises for special-needs children.

Yoga for Teens by Thia Luby. Santa Fe, New Mexico: Clear Light Publishers, 1999. Benefits of doing yoga during the teen years. Includes both basic and more advanced poses.

Yoga Journal's Yoga Basics by Mara Carrico and the Editors of Yoga Journal. New York: Henry Holt and Company, 1997. For adults, but the instructions for the poses are clear and easy to follow, with good photographs.

Websites

www.childrensyoga.com
Geared toward young children. Includes poses, yoga games, information for parents and teachers, and assistance in finding a yoga teacher.

www.nextgenerationyoga.com
A New York yoga studio founded specifically for kids.

www.specialyoga.com
Advice and information for parents of special-needs children. Includes a newsletter, a list of certified teachers in the U.S. and internationally, and links to related websites.

www.sportsite.com.ar/yogaorganizations.html
A directory of international, continental, and national yoga organizations, with links to most of them.

www.yogafinder.com
Helps you find yoga classes and teachers throughout the world. Also lists yoga events and has a catalogue of products.

www.yogajournal.com
Website of *Yoga Journal* magazine.

Magazines

Yoga Journal
2054 University Avenue, Suite 600
Berkeley, California, USA 94704
www.yogajournal.com
Articles about poses, interviews with celebrities who do yoga, yoga philosophy, meditation, healthy eating, etc. Back pages list suppliers of yoga clothing and products. *Yoga Journal* also produces a series of yoga videos and DVDs, which can be ordered on-line.

Yoga International Magazine
RR1, Box 1130
Honesdale, PA 18431-9718
www.yimag.org
How yoga is practiced around the world, poses, yoga philosophy, health, etc. Includes a service for finding a yoga teacher and an e-mail exchange where you can talk to other yoga practitioners.

Glossary

Affirmation: a positive thought or statement such as "I can do this pose" or "I am tall and centered"

Asanas (ah-SAH-naz): the poses of hatha yoga; from the Sanskrit meaning "a posture comfortably held"

Ashtanga yoga (ash-TANG-a): a style of hatha yoga often called "power yoga," in which the postures are done rapidly and forcefully to build strength

Bhagavad Gita (BAH-gah-vad GEE-ta): the sacred text of the Hindu religion

Ma Jaya Sati Bhagavati (ma JIE-a SAH-tee bah-gah-VAH-tee): a famous yogi who cares for people who are terminally ill

Bhakti (BOCK-tee) **yoga**: one of the six branches of yoga; the path of devotion

Bikram yoga: a style of hatha yoga that is done in a hot humid room to loosen the muscles; not considered healthy for children

Indra Devi: a famous yogi who is credited with spreading hatha yoga across America

Guru: someone who teaches yoga; from the Sanskrit *gu*, "darkness," and *ru*, "light"; a master who leads us out of the darkness of ignorance into the light of knowledge

Hatha yoga: one of the six branches of yoga; the path of physical mastery; the yoga of the poses

Integral yoga: a style of hatha yoga that tries to blend postures, relaxation, breathing, and meditation into a person's entire life

Inverted: upside-down; refers to yoga postures that reverse the body's usual position, such as Downward Facing Dog and Shoulder Stand

Iyengar (eye-YEN-gar) **yoga**: a style of hatha yoga that emphasizes the proper placement of the body

Jnana (GYAN-a) **yoga**: one of the six branches of yoga; the path of wisdom

Karma yoga: one of the six branches of yoga; the path of service

Kundalini (kun-da-LEE-nee) **yoga**: a style of hatha yoga that uses breath, postures, chanting, and meditation to awaken and release the energy stored at the base of the spine

Mantra: a word or sound that is chanted, either aloud or silently, to focus the mind; also, a form of tantra yoga

Meditation: a practice in which you try to empty your mind of extra thoughts and focus it inward, in order to reach an inner place of concentration and stillness

Om: a mystical sound thought to contain all the sounds of the universe

Patanjali (pah-tan-JAH-lee): an Indian sage who lived around 200 BC and is considered the founder of yoga

Prana (PRAH-nah): a Sanskrit word meaning "breath" or "life force"

Pranayama (prah-nah-YAH-ma): the breathing practices of yoga; from the Sanskrit *prana*, "breath or life force," and *ayama*, "extension"

Prone: lying face-down; yoga postures done facing the floor, either on your hands and knees or on your stomach, such as Cobra and Cat

Raja yoga: one of the six branches of yoga; the path of inner focus or meditation

Swami Rama: a famous yogi who took part in medical experiments using yoga techniques

Ramakrishna (rah-mah-KRISH-na): a famous yogi who taught that many paths lead to God

Sage: a wise, learned person

Samadhi (SAHM-dee): the goal of meditation; a state of pure joy in which the self unites with God

Sanjna (SANJ-a-na): the wife of Surya, the Hindu Sun god

Sanskrit: an ancient Indian language

Soma (SOE-ma): the Hindu Moon god

Sufis (SOO-fees): a sect of Islamic mystics

Supine: lying face-up; yoga postures done lying on the back, such as Knee Hug and Bridge

Surya (SOOR-ya): the Hindu Sun god

Sutra (SOO-tra): from the Sanskrit meaning "thread"; a saying that expresses a profound truth in just a few words

Swami: a title of respect given to a spiritual master of yoga

Tantra yoga: one of the six branches of yoga; the path of ritual; includes mantra yoga

Viniyoga: a style of hatha yoga that puts the emphasis on the breath

Visualization: a practice in which you imagine peaceful or positive mind pictures

Yoga: from the Sanskrit meaning "yoke" or "union"; a system of movements, breathing exercises, and relaxation techniques designed to unite the body, mind, and spirit

Paramahansa Yogananda (par-ma-HAN-sa yo-ga-NAN-da): a famous yogi who taught that yoga blends with the principles of all true religions

Yogi: a person who practices yoga; often used to refer to a yoga teacher

Yogin: a male yogi

Yogini: a female yogi

Yoga Asanas